Mission Statements for College Libraries

2nd Edition

CLIP Note #28

Compiled by

Jamie A Hastreiter
Eckerd College
St. Petersburg, Florida

Marsha Cornelius
Stetson University
Deland, Florida

David W. Henderson
Eckerd College
St. Petersburg, Florida

College Library Information Packet Committee
College Libraries Section
Association of College and Research Libraries
A Division of the American Library Association
Chicago 1999

The paper used in this publication meets the minimum requirements of American National Standard for Information Sciences–Permanence of Paper for Printed Library Materials, ANSI Z39.48-1992. ∞

Library of Congress Cataloging-in-Publication Data
Mission statements for college libraries / compiled by Jamie A.
    Hastreiter, Marsha Cornelius, David W. Henderson. -- 2nd ed.
            p. cm. -- (CLIP note : #28)
        Rev. ed. of: Mission statements for college libraries / Larry
    Hardesty, 1985.
        Includes bibliographical references.
        ISBN 0-8389-8047-3 (alk. paper)
        1. Academic libraries--Aims and objectives--United States.
    2. Mission statements--United States. I. Hastreiter, Jamie.
    II. Cornelius, Marsha. III. Henderson, David, 1945– .
    IV. Hardesty, Larry L. Mission statements for college libraries.
    V. Series: CLIP notes ; #28.
    Z675.U5M556 1999
    027.7'0973--dc21   99-34722

Printed on recycled paper.

Printed in the United States of America.

03 02 01 00 99   5 4 3 2

TABLE OF CONTENTS

Private Institutions With Over 2500 students

CLIP Notes Committee

Lewis R. Miller, Chair
Irwin Library
Butler University
Indianapolis, IN

Roxann Bustos
Reese Library
Augusta College
Augusta, Georgia

Jody L. Caldwell
Drew University Libraries
Drew University
Madison, NJ

Doralyn H. Edwards
Fondren Library
Rice University
Houston, TX

Jamie Hastreiter
William Luther Cobb Library
Eckerd College
St. Petersburg, FL

Jennifer Taxman
Lucy Scribner Library
Skidmore College
Saratoga Springs, NY

Mickey Zemon
Emerson College Library
Emerson College
Boston, MA

Introduction

Objective

The *College Library Information Packet (CLIP) Note* publishing program strives to provide college and small university libraries with a method of sharing policies and documentation. The intent of this *CLIP Note* is to provide data and sample documents that can be used as examples by institutions that are writing or rewriting their mission statements.

The first recommendation in the 1995 *Standards for College Libraries* outlines the need to have a written statement of purpose. Various accreditation agencies also require a written statement relating the mission of the library to the mission of the parent institution. This *CLIP Note* shows that a majority of the academic libraries surveyed are in compliance with those recommendations.

Background

In 1985, two of the authors, along with Larry Hardesty, undertook a study of mission statements, which resulted in the publication of *CLIP Notes #5 Mission Statements for College Libraries*. The focus then was on whether the impact of economic strains on college budgets was a primary force in mission statement development. Budgets were being strained by rapidly rising periodical costs. Online searching and the use of computer software were relatively new services that libraries were attempting to squeeze into their already tight budgets.

The present focus in studying mission statements is to examine the impact that rapidly changing technologies have had on the creation or modification of mission statements. Have libraries seen a need to reexamine their mission as it relates to the overall mission of their parent institution? Over the last decade, an increased emphasis on automation, interconnectivity, distance education, and organizational restructuring, in many instances, has altered the view of the traditional library. Although libraries have had to respond to the advances brought about by technology, have they responded with corresponding revisions to their mission statements?

Now, as then, our goal is to gather data and examples of documentation relevant to the purposes of academic libraries. Such documents may be referred to as goal statements, library philosophy, statements of purpose, or statements of objectives. Responses from libraries also indicate that "mission statements" may be developed as a separate statement or as part of a more narrowly focused policy, such as the collection development policy. Whatever the case, a majority of libraries surveyed have felt the need to prepare a statement that defines their purpose in some meaningful way.

There are many similarities with the results of the 1985 survey. For instance, there is still a wide range of mission statements: some only a sentence or two, while others are quite lengthy. The library director, librarians, and library staff are still the primary contributors to the development and adoption of mission statements.

Survey Procedure

The authors used the standard procedure for all *CLIP Notes*, with the exception that they used the 1985 mission statement survey as a foundation for questions. That allows comparisons to be made between the results of the first and second edition. To deal with technology and the advances that have impacted libraries in the last decade, the authors added questions on electronic materials and web access. The survey was drafted and sent to the *CLIP Notes* Committee of the Association of College and Research Libraries (ACRL) College Library Section for revision and approval.

The survey was mailed in April 1998 to the 268 library directors at college and small universities which have agreed to participate in this project. The surveyed libraries include institutions classified by the Carnegie Foundation for the Advancement of Teaching as Baccalaureate I or II or MA I or II. Reminder postcards were sent in June 1998 to institutions that did not respond. The return rate was 60% with 161 libraries responding.

Analysis of Survey Results

Institutional Information

The institutions that responded to the survey were primarily (79.5%) private. Most of these libraries operate as an independent unit. Only 2 of the 33 public institution libraries and 11 of the 126 private institution libraries are part of a larger unit. This shows that, of the participating libraries, few have merged their library with another unit, such as the Computer Center/Institutional Technology department. Interestingly, the surveyed libraries have nearly the same average number of FTE students and librarians as those that responded in 1985. Average numbers of book volumes and print periodical subscriptions show a decrease since 1985, but budget figures have risen.

Eighty-five percent of the reporting libraries have a mission statement. This figure is significantly higher than the 56% reported in the 1985 survey. Institutions reporting no mission statement numbered 21 private and 2 public academic libraries. The increase in libraries with mission statements is significant. The compilers speculate that the 29% increase is the result of greater emphasis by accrediting agencies, increased budgetary demands, or reorganization of departments. Our small sample keeps us from drawing too many far-reaching conclusions about this increase.

There appears to be no correlation between size and whether or not a library has a mission statement. Schools reporting no mission statement had an average of 2,218 students and 6 FTE librarians. Neither figure is very different from the average for all institutions. Comparisons of the size of the collection are slightly significant. Libraries with no mission statement ranged from 70,000 to 480,000 volumes with a median of 157,500 volumes. Libraries with a mission statement had a range of 54,800 to 1,201,262 with a median of 182,882 volumes. However, a comparison of libraries with mission statements to those without differ very little in the median number of online/CD-ROM titles (20 to 27), the number of electronic journals (1000 each), or the number of print titles (1016 to 1000). (The median is cited because it gives a more accurate picture of the data received.)

Total budget for those libraries reporting a mission statement was higher than for those with no mission statement. The median budget for those with a mission statement was $873,767 while those without was $640,000. The median amount reported for online/CD-ROM expenditures was higher for those with no mission statement ($24,600 to $22,500). The median expenditure for electronic serials was also higher for those libraries without mission statements, $18,500 versus $17,200. The median amount spent on print journals, however, was higher for libraries with a mission statement ($140,700 versus $90,000).

Reporting libraries have different ways of allocating funds for electronic purchases. Several librarians reported that they combined print and electronic serials purchases in one account. Others have an "electronic materials" budget line which covers all online and CD-ROM expenditures, and, in some cases, includes AV materials. Some libraries include CD-ROMs in the monograph budget. As electronic formats assume a more prominent position in the library, a true accounting of the amount spent on them may become necessary to provide a real picture of how library funds are divided.

No conclusions could be drawn from the answers to the question about the number of electronic journals. This question gave respondents trouble. Certainly, ascertaining an exact figure is like trying to hit a moving target. Database providers are constantly updating their content list and adding additional database packages. One respondent was "unable to count, but it's a lot." Some respondents listed databases to which they subscribed, but not the number of fulltext titles included in the databases. Another said there was overlap in the titles on various databases that was not adjusted. How important is it for librarians to know how many titles are accessible at their institution, and how much overlap exists in databases? Is the information necessary for evaluation? Is the effort expended in checking titles worth it in the end?

<u>Mission Statement Review and Development</u> (Questions 11-13)

Over one-quarter of the respondents revise their mission statements, as broadly defined, each year. For another one quarter of the respondents, the accreditation process is a motivating force for rewriting the mission statement with revision intervals ranging from 5-10 years. To the "other" category, 22 out of 59 (37%) respondents listed specific intervals of 2 to 10 years between revisions. Linking revision to long range planning, grants, annual planning, review of the parent institution's mission statement, rewriting of the collection development policy, or program review accounted for 10 (17%) of the responses.

Nearly 34% of the respondents (20) revise their mission statement irregularly. Presumably, in these cases, something acts as a trigger, such as a change in director or a change in the institution, which causes the mission statement to become a priority. One respondent reported 10 years between revisions, but commented that "practically speaking" it could be qualified as never. Building on this, we can say that 27 respondents (43%) do not see revising their mission statement as a priority, since they responded that they irregularly or never evaluate their mission statement. Nonetheless, over 85% (116) have revised their document in the last 10 years. Another 12 respondents recognize a need to do so, or commented they were in the midst of such an evaluation.

<u>Groups Involved in Mission Statement Development</u> (Questions 14-19)

The library director, librarians, and library staff are the main groups involved in developing mission statements, being listed 349 times by respondents. Where a committee was used, the library director and librarians either gave the charge or chaired the committee in almost 40% of the cases. Where no committee was used, the library staff again was heavily involved in writing the mission statement with the library director or another librarian listed as the author in almost 72% of the responses. In the "other" category, library staff members were almost entirely credited with the authorship of the mission statement. The majority of respondents (75%) took less than four months to write and adopt their mission statement. The main bodies that adopt or approve mission statements are the librarians and library staff and the chief academic officer. The faculty library committee or advisory library committee was the third most popular answer. Two respondents said that formal adoption was not necessary.

Importance of Mission Statements (Questions 20-24)

Ninety-six percent of the respondents felt that working on a mission statement was worth the effort, and believed that other librarians felt that mission statements were important, although to a slightly lesser degree (89%). A majority (71%) felt that administrators thought mission statements were important. Sixty percent of the respondents either thought teaching faculty found mission statements unimportant or they had no opinion about faculty beliefs. These statistics mirror the figures found in the 1985 survey.

All respondents answered that copies of the mission statement are available in print or electronic form. How they were made available varied greatly. Print copies were often part of another document: a self-study, library guide, collection development policy, library policy handbook, institution publications, or long range plan. Many commented that the mission statement is distributed to faculty, administrators and library committee members. A few respondents make it available only on request. In addition to the 58 respondents who post it on the campus network or library homepage, another 11 replied that they intend to post it on a homepage at some point in the future. Several of those eleven people gave this survey credit for making them decide to put it on their homepage. One unusual reply stated that "Students asked to remove it from webpage."

Libraries Without Mission Statements (Questions 25-30)

The chief answers as to why a library does not have a mission statement are that they are too general to be useful, that they use the parent institution's mission statement, and that they are generally ignored. The most cited reasons for not developing a mission statement are that they are too general, that they seldom are useful in getting more funding, and that they are too time consuming to prepare. This parallels responses to the 1985 survey. The majority of respondents have never been asked for a mission statement by an accreditation association.

Respondents were divided in their response to the question of how important a mission statement is to their libraries. Twelve (52%) thought it was important or very important, while eleven (48%) thought it was not important or had no opinion. A majority of these respondents either felt teaching faculty and administrators did not think mission statements are important or they had no opinion. These findings are also similar to the responses to the 1985 survey. If librarians feel that other campus groups do not value mission statements, there is little push to develop one.

Conclusion

In the final analysis, over the past fifteen years more college libraries have recognized the usefulness of developing and/or revising their mission statements. The impetus for and methods used in developing these statements, however, have changed little. When librarians perceive them to be important, whether as a response to outside requirements or simply as an aid in defining the institutional/library culture, mission statements are conceived. Perhaps the best reasons for developing mission statements can be found in the following comments from two respondents. "The mission statement is important to our university and to our profession.... The mission statement is always in front of us as we write our yearly strategic goals." "A mission or vision statement should not be just eloquent words but should serve as a star to steer by. It can and should be a guide for program and resource decisions: how would this further our mission? If it wouldn't, then we shouldn't do it, or we should revise the mission."

Selected Bibliography

BIBLIOGRAPHY

American Library Association. "Administrative Policies and Procedures Affecting Access to Library Resources and Services". In *Intellectual Freedom Manual*, 3rd ed. Washington, D.C.: American Library Association, 1989.

Bangert, Stephanie Rogers. "Values in College and University Library Mission Statements: A Search for Distinctive Beliefs, Meaning, and Organizational Culture." *Advances in Librarianship* 21 (1997): 91-106.

Billington, James H. "Statement of James H. Billington, the Librarian of Congress, before the Joint Committee on the Library, October 4". *Library of Congress Information Bulletin* 47 (1988): 423-7.

Breuer, James E. "Managing the Growth." *Inform* 4 (Nov./Dec. 1990): 32-4.

Brophy, Peter. "The Mission of the Academic Library." *British Journal of Academic Librarianship*, 6.3 (1991): 135-47.

DeCandido, GraceAnne Andreassi. "Your Mission, Should You Choose to Accept It." *Wilson Library Bulletin* 69 (March 1995): 6.

Hardesty, Larry L., Jamie Hastreiter, and David Henderson. *Mission Statements for College Libraries*. CLIP Notes #5. Chicago: ACRL/ALA, 1985.

_____. "Development of College Library Mission Statements." *Journal of Library Administration* 9.3 (1988): 11-34.

"Library of Congress in the Year 2000: A Vision." *Information Reports and Bibliographies* 18.1 (1989): 22-3.

"MAP (Management and Planning) Committee Issues Vision Statement for Discussion." *Library of Congress Information Bulletin* 47 (1988): 311-13.

Mosley, Madison M. "Mission Statements for the Community College LRC." *College and Research Libraries News* 10 (1988): 653-4.

Nash, Laura. "Mission Statements: Mirrors and Windows." *Harvard Business Review* 88 (March-April 1988): 155.

"A Revitalized Philosophy." *The School Librarian's Workshop* 11 (Feb. 1991):
13.

Robinson, Susan Rathbun. "Library Mission and Codes of Ethics: A Content
Analysis of Research Library Policy Documents and their Ethical
Premises." Master's Thesis, University of North Carolina at Chapel Hill,
1994.

"Standards for College Libraries." *College & Research Libraries News* 56
(1995): 248.

Woods, L.B. "Mission Statements, Organizational Goals, and Objectives.
Arkansas Libraries 45 (June 1988): 13-17.

CLIP *Note* Survey Results

Association of College & Research Libraries
College Libraries Section
CLIP NOTE SURVEY

Mission Statements for College Libraries

The following survey is designed to gather information regarding the development of College Library Mission Statements and to inquire about the impetus for their revision.

---

161 respondents out of 268 surveys for a 60% return.

 Institutional Information

Type of Institution: *(check one)*　　**33 (20.5%)**　Public　　**128 (79.5%)**　Private

Number of full-time equivalent (FTE) students:　　　　　**152 respondents**
　　　　Range: 554-7900　　　　**Average: 2418**　　**Median: 2023**

Number of full-time equivalent (FTE) faculty:　　　　　**147 respondents**
　　　　Range: 5-643　　　　**Average: 153**　　**Median: 140**

Regional Accreditation Agency: *(check one)*　　　　**161 respondents**
36 (22%)　Middle States Association　　**17 (11%)**　New England Association
60 (37%)　North Central Association　　**9 (6%)**　Northwest Association
34 (21%)　Southern Association　　　　**5 (3%)**　Western Association

1) Which best describes your library's position in the campus organization
　　structure? *(check one)*　　　　　　　　　　　**159 respondents**
145 (91%)　a) Operates as an independent unit.
　0 (0%)　b) Merged with the Computer Center.
　13 (8%)　c) Operates independently but is part of a larger unit such
　　　　　　　　as Information Technology department.
　1 (1%)　d) Other (please specify) - **Includes AV services**

**All Figures Requested are for Fall 1997
or Fiscal Year 1997-98**

 **Library Size**

2) Number of full-time equivalent (FTE) personnel in your library: **158 respondents**
   a) Librarians: **Range: 1-22**   **Average: 7**   **Median: 6**
   b) Staff: **Range: 1-50**   **Average: 10.8**   **Median: 9**

3) Approximate number of book volumes, excluding bound periodicals, in your library: **153 respondents**
   Range: 54,800-1,201,262   **Average: 226,054**   **Median: 180,000**

4) Approximate number of Online/CD-ROM titles, e.g. encyclopedias, indexes, reference guides (excluding full-text journals counted below):   **141 respondents**
   Range: 0-2689   **Average: 147**   **Median: 32**

5) Approximate number of current print periodical subscriptions: **156 respondents**
   Range: 225-3546   **Average: 1164**   **Median: 1060**

6) Approximate number of journals accessible electronically (individually or through IAC, Ebscohost, etc.):   **133 respondents**
   Range: 0-30,000   **Average: 2117**   **Median: 1200**

💰 Library Budget

7) Approximate total budget for your library: **156 respondents**
   Range: $65,000-$4,878,900   **Average: $1,090,057** **Median: $825,000**

8) Approximate total library materials expenditures for your library:
                                                                   151 respondents
   Range: $35,000-$1,804,685   **Average: $398,979**   **Median: $308,562**

9) a) Approximate monograph expenditure: **156 respondents**
      Range: $5,000-$666,794   **Average: $144,946**   **Median: $104,508**

   b) Approximate On-line/CD-ROM expenditure (non-journal):   **126 respondents**
      Range: $0-$2,853,150   **Average: $46,142**   **Median: $24,000**

   c) Approximate serials expenditure:
      Print: **144 respondents**
      Range: $6,500-$952,000   **Average: $171,314**   **Median: $138,840**
      Electronic: **81 respondents**
      Range: $0-$219,150   **Average: $15,392**   **Median: $17,200**

d) Other materials expenditure: *(please specify)*   **59 respondents**
    AV/videos/film/media (54)   **ILL/Document delivery (8)**
    Microforms (28)   **Computer search (3)**
    Binding/Preservation (19)   **Software/CDs (6)**

Mission Statement Information

10) Has your library developed a Mission Statement, Statement of Objectives, or
    similar statement? *(check one)*   **162 respondents***
    *One respondent had 2 answers

136 **(84%)** Yes (please answer questions 10 through 23)
  2   **(1%)**   Library's mission is included in Mission Statement of department
                    overseeing the library.
 24 **(15%)** No (please skip to question 24)

Please send a copy of your Mission Statement.

---

11) How often is Mission Statement reviewed? *(check one)*   **134 respondents**
38 **(28%)** a) Annually
34 **(25%)** b) In conjunction with accreditation process (specify frequency)
                    2-3 years (9)   **3 years (1)**
                    5 years (9)   **5-10 (12)**
                    7-10 years (2)   **10 years (8)**
59 **(44%)** c) Other (please specify)
                    As needed/irregularly (20)   **For strategic planning (6)**
                    Every 5 years (12)   **Every 2-3 years (9)**
                    When get new director (3)   **When other documents are (4)**
                    Every 10 years (1)
  4   **(3%)** d) Never

12) Has your library's Mission Statement been revised in the last 10 years?
    (check one)   **134 respondents**
116 **(87%)** Yes   If yes, in what year   **Range: 1989-1998**
 18 **(13%)** No   If no, do you see a need to reexamine your Mission
                    Statement in light of changing circumstances?
                    12 (67%) Yes   **6 (33%) No**

13) Which of the following were motivating factors in the development of your Mission Statement? *Please rank in order of importance with 1 being the most important and 10 being the least important.*

*Figures were adjusted by the average of items not ranked   **132 respondents**

Avg 2.8 a) Reevaluation and/or reorganization of library objectives
Avg 5.4 b) Change in institutional mission
Avg 6.0 c) Reorganization of institutional units, e.g. library/computer center
Avg 4.9 d) Desire to comply with "Standards for College Libraries"
Avg 3.9 e) Accreditation needs
Avg 4.0 f) Advances in technology
Avg 6.1 g) Distance learning
Avg 5.9 h) Change in client base, e.g. more adult learners, open to public
2 replies i) Do not know
             j) Other *(please specify)*

New director (9)	**Planning new library (3)**
Strategic planning (7)	**Address user needs (3)**
Had none before (4)	**Put on web page (2)**
Clarify goals for staff (3)	

14) Who was involved in the development of your Mission Statement?
     (check all that apply)   **136 respondents**

133 **(98%)** a) Library Director
 63 **(46%)** b) Assistant Director(s) and/or Senior Librarians
117 **(86%)** c) Librarians
 33 **(24%)** d) *Classroom Faculty Member(s)*
 42 **(31%)** e) Administrator(s) (specify titles)

> **Dean of Faculty/Provost/Academic VP (30)**
> **President (4)**   **Registrar (1)**
> **President's Administrative Council (1)**

 25 **(18%)** f) Student(s)
 50 **(37%)** g) Others (specify)

> **Library staff (36)**
> **Faculty/Advisory Library Committee (17)**
> **Students on library committees (3)**
> **Board of Trustees/Regents (2)**
> **External evaluators/library directors (2)**

15) If a committee was used, was it: *(check all that apply)*

If no committee was used, skip to question #25.

74 respondents

26	**(35%)**	a)	A regular faculty library committee
25	**(34%)**	b)	A special committee formed for this purpose
7	**(10%)**	c)	Other (please specify)

    Librarians/library staff (3)
    Library building committee (1)
    Strategic plan task force (1)

0	**(0%)**	d)	Chaired by the Information Technology Director
33	**(45%)**	e)	Chaired by the Library Director
10	**(14%)**	f)	Chaired by a Librarian (specify title)

    Public Services Librarian (2)
    Systems Librarian (1)
    ILL/Documents Librarian (1)
    Catalog Librarian/Music Catalog Librarian (2)

11	**(15%)**	g)	Chaired by a Classroom Faculty Member
5	**(7%)**	h)	Other (please specify)

    Entire staff (3)
    Trustee (1)
    Librarians Advisory Council (1)

2	**(2.7%)**	i)	Given a charge by the Information Technology Director
21	**(28%)**	j)	Given a charge by the Library Director
9	**(12%)**	k)	Given a charge by an Administrator (specify title)

    Vice-President of Academic Affairs/Provost (5)
    President (2)
    Sr. Vice-President (1)

2	**(3%)**	l)	Given a charge by another Committee
2	**(3%)**	m)	No charge given
8	**(11%)**	n)	Other (please specify)

    Entire staff (2)
    Library faculty (2)
    Outside consultant (1)
    Activity of Library Policy & Planning Group(1)

16) If no committee was used, who wrote the statement? *(check all that apply)*

70 respondents

55 **(79%)** a) Library Director
  9 **(13%)** b) Another Librarian (please specify title)
                  Public Services Librarian (1)
                  Technical Services Librarian (1)
                  Reference Librarian (1)
                  Information Services Librarian (1)
                  Collection Development (2)
                  Instructional Services (1)
  3 **(2%)** c) Administrator (please specify title)
                  Dean of Faculty (1)
                  IE Director (1)
  0 **(0%)** d) Classroom Faculty Member
22 **(31%)** e) Other (please specify)
                  Collaborative/group/entire staff effort (17)
                  Librarians and Director (4)
                  Consultant/Counselor/Facilitator (3)
                  Library Governance group (librarians & elected staff) (1)

17) Was the Mission Statement formally adopted or approved by the:
    (check all that apply)

135 respondents

90 **(67%)** a) Librarians
14 **(10%)** b) Faculty Senate or equivalent
66 **(49%)** c) Chief Academic Officer (Dean, Provost, Vice-president of
             Academic Affairs, or equivalent)
16 **(12%)** d) President
 6 (2.31%) e) Board of Trustees or equivalent
  0 **(0%)** f) Student Government
43 **(32%)** g) Other (please specify)
                  Library Committee/Council (22)
                  Library Staff (13)
                  Associate Provost (1)
                  President's Advisory (1)
                  Dean's Council (1)
25 **(19%)** h) Never formally adopted or approved

18) Approximately how long did it take to develop the Mission Statement from
    initial draft to adoption? *(check one)*   **135 respondents**
    *Some respondents gave more than one answer.

13 **(10%)** a) Less than a week
40 **(30%)** b) A week to less than a month
47 **(35%)** c) A month to less than four months
18 **(13%)** d) Four months to less than an academic year
10 **(7%)**   e) An academic year
 4 **(3%)**   f) More than an academic year (please specify)
                       Year and a half
 5 **(4%)**   g) Do not know

19) How is your Mission Statement used? *Please rank in order of importance
    with 1 being the most important and 10 being the least important.*

Avg 3.8 a) To guide improvement of services.
Avg 4.9 b) To guide collection development.
Avg 7.3 c) To guide expansion of staff.
Avg 7.1 d) To guide reallocation of staff.
Avg 7.3 e) To guide improvement of the physical plant.
Avg 3.5 f) To relate the purpose of the library to the objectives of the teaching
                 faculty.
Avg 4.4 g) To relate the purpose of the library to objectives of the college
                 administrators.
Avg 3.6 h) To relate the purpose of the library to student needs.
Avg 5.6 i) To relate the purpose of the library to the accreditation requirements
                 of outside evaluators.
Avg 7.5 j) Other (please specify)
                 For future planning (9)
                 To relate purpose of the library to college mission (7)
                 To provide clarity and direction for library employees/services (6)
                 Part of annual self-evaluation and goal setting (5)
                 Part of annual budget review (3)
                 Core course in Information Literacy taught by librarians (1)

20) In your opinion, was the effort expended in developing the Mission
    Statement worthwhile? *(check one)*   **136 respondents**
66 **(49%)** a) Very worthwhile
64 **(47%)** b) Worthwhile
 2 **(2%)**   c) Not worthwhile
 4 **(3%)**   d) No opinion

21) In your opinion, how important is the Mission Statement to the librarians at your institution? *(check one)* **135 respondents**

37 **(27%)** a) Very important
84 **(62%)** b) Important
14 **(10%)** c) Not important
0 **(0%)** d) No opinion

22) In your opinion, how important is the Mission Statement to the teaching faculty at your institution? *(check one)* **136 respondents**

7 **(5%)** a) Very important
47 **(35%)** b) Important
66 **(49%)** c) Not important
16 **(12%)** d) No opinion

23) In your opinion, how important is the Mission Statement to the administrators at your institution? *(check one)* **136 respondents**

28 **(21%)** a) Very important
68 **(50%)** b) Important
28 **(21%)** c) Not important
11 **(8%)** d) No opinion

24) In which manner do you make your Mission Statement available to your administrators, faculty, and clientele in general? *(check all that apply)* **134 respondents**

68 **(51%)** a) Print copies available in library
42 **(31%)** b) Printed in college publication
17 **(13%)** c) Posted on campus network (intranet)
41 **(31%)** d) Posted on library homepage (internet) URL: _____
32 **(24%)** e) Other *(Please specify)*
               Self study documents/ Long range plan/Annual report (7)
               Distributed to administrators/faculty/committees (8)
               Part of library guide (1)
               Library Policies & Procedures Manual/
               Collection Development Policy (5)
               Library newsletter (1)
               Given to staff (4)
               Told to freshmen (1)
               Student handbook (1)
               Provided as needed (6)
               Will put on homepage (10)
               Various library and institution publications (2)

> **REMEMBER to enclose a copy of your Mission Statement.**
> **Now skip to page 8 for your comments and further instructions.**

Libraries Without Mission Statements

25) Which of the following reasons may be factors as to why your library does not have a Mission Statement? *(check all that apply)*   **23 respondents**

4 **(17%)** a) Mission Statements are too time consuming to create.

1 **(4%)** b) Mission Statements are too political. *(please explain)*
"We should have one and we've mentioned one occasionally. Probably a question of time vs priorities."

10 **(44%)** c) Mission Statements are too general to be useful.

6 **(26%)** d) Mission Statements are usually ignored by everyone.

0 **(0%)** e) Mission Statements unnecessarily limit the role and activities of the library.

5 **(22%)** f) Mission Statements are seldom useful in obtaining additional library funds.

2 **(9%)** g) Mission Statements seldom take into account the level of resources available to the library.

0 **(0%)** h) Development of Mission Statements create divisive arguments.

2 **(9%)** i) Library's mission is given as part of a larger Information Technology or other department statement.

15 **(65%)** j) Other (please specify)
Follow that institutions mission statement (7)
No time (3)
In the process of developing one (1)
The collection development policy covers the same ground (1)
Too vague, too theoretical (1)
Librarians are waiting for College to acknowledge ACRL standards (1)

26) Has an accreditation association ever asked for or recommended the development of a Mission Statement or similar statement for your library? *(check one)*   **23 respondents**

2 **(9%)** Yes

17 **(74%)** No

4 **(17%)** Do not know

27) How important is the development of a library mission statement to you? *(check one)*   **23 respondents**

2 **(9%)** a) Very important

10 **(43%)** b) Important

9 **(39%)** c) Not important

2 **(9%)** d) No opinion

28) How important is the development of a library Mission Statement to other librarians at your institution? *(check one)* **21 respondents**

0 **(0%)** a) Very important
10 **(48%)** b) Important
9 **(43%)** c) Not important
2 **(10%)** d) No opinion

29) How important is the development of a library Mission Statement to the teaching faculty at your institution? *(check one)* **23 respondents**

0 **(0%)** a) Very important
1 **(4%)** b) Important
15 **(65%)** c) Not important
7 **(30%)** d) No opinion

30) How important is the development of a library Mission Statement to the administrators at your institution? *(check one)* **23 respondents**

0 **(0%)** a) Very important
5 **(22%)** b) Important
13 **(57%)** c) Not important
5 **(22%)** d) No opinion

 Your Comments:

As a result of receiving this questionnaire, my awareness was raised for the need to review the Mission Statement in light of a new organization and new technologies.

We have just completed a process of developing a new vision/mission for Albion College. This process convinced us that the library must see itself as an integral part of our institution's mission and that it was important to us to develop program goals and objectives that were closely coordinated with and integral to this mission. Our planning process within the library begins with the Institutional Vision Statement, Core Values, & Statement of Purpose document and builds program goals to achieve and match this agenda.

The mission of the library is frequently held up to the staff. Proposed policies and actions usually must answer the question "How does this meet our mission?" We also conducted a task analysis with the central question, "Does this task help us meet our mission?"

A mission or vision statement should not be just eloquent words but should serve as a star to steer by. It can and should be a guide for program and resource decisions:

How would this further our mission? If it wouldn't, then we shouldn't do it, or we should revise the mission.

The mission statement is important to our university and to our profession. Our inclusion of our AL Code of Ethics and the Right to Read clarifies the library profession to our users. The Mission Statement is always in front of us as we write our yearly strategic goals.

Our entire staff was engaged in defining our vision and the initiatives on which we would base our development of services and annual outcomes assessment. This process laid the groundwork for the campus adoption of a library building program in this planning cycle.

The Weiss Library mission statement is very simple and was intended to provide a base out of which goals and objectives would flow. It has been reviewed but not rewritten. The librarians will be taking a hard look at it in the next few months as (1) consideration is given to building a new library or renovating and adding on to the present building and (2) the college expands its non-traditional programs to include more distance learning.

Basic use of the mission statement is to shoot down the occasional off-the-wall brainstorm from an administrator or faculty member.

Everything should flow from the mission statement: That is how you provide materials and services in a timely, effective, and efficient manner. The mission should guide materials selection, deselection, and preservation. In dealing with classroom faculty and with administration, the mission is the librarian's greatest ally. Our mission statement is integrated in our collection development policy.

I personally think too much time is wasted on the development of mission statements and not enough on their implementation.

We also developed a vision statement which helps guide our activities. Together they and other campus documents help us shape and revise our shorter term strategic goals.

Writing a mission statement was an experience that brought our faculty and staff together with common goals.

A mission statement alone isn't enough. It needs to be supported by statements of the library staff's values and statements ("missions") of each section of the library.

We plan to revise in light of online technology & distance learning. But the main emphasis does not need much changing. How we do things has changed. What we do has not.

Survey Results 23

Mission Statement Documents

Private Institutions

Under 2500 Students

Herrick Memorial Library
Mission and Vision Statement

Mission:

We at Herrick Memorial Library believe in the leadership potential of Alfred University students. We know that responsible leadership requires the ability to use information wisely in making decisions.

Therefore, we commit ourselves to ensuring that students at Alfred University have the opportunity and freedom to learn to access, evaluate, and use the information they need while practicing the art of responsible leadership.

Strategies:

We will accomplish our mission by:

- Treating every encounter as a learning opportunity.
- Promoting, encouraging, and nurturing information literacy skills.
- Focusing on continuous improvement of service quality.
- Providing seamless access to information resources within Herrick Library and worldwide.
- Serving our patrons with enthusiasm, sensitivity, and intellectual honesty, giving priority to their needs.
- Stepping forward to meet the challenges posed by information technology.
- Practicing and supporting innovative thinking, flexibility, and openness to change.
- Fostering respect and trust to maximize effective cooperation, communication, and collaboration.
- Creating a comfortable, attractive place for studying and conveniently accessing information.
- Encouraging and supporting on-going training and staff development at all levels to prepare staff for managing multiple responsibilities, achieving technological competence, and acquiring new skills to enhance the depth of library experience in which we take pride.

http://www.herr.alfred.edu/staff/mission.htm

Augustana College

The Augustana College Library serves the needs of the Augustana College community. The Library clientele consists of the student, faculty and staff populations. The Library provides additional support to the Graduate Center, and is open to the public.

The mission of the Augustana College Library supports the mission statement of the College. The Library considers itself a vital component of the educational process, and thus stands behind the following statements which have been ratified by the Library Committee and Faculty Senate.

AUGUSTANA COLLEGE LIBRARY MISSION STATEMENT

INFORMATION IS THE KEY TO SUCCESSFUL LIVING. ■ EDUCATION IS A LIFELONG ENDEAVOR. ■ THE **AUGUSTANA COLLEGE LIBRARY** IS AWARE OF THE VALUE OF INFORMATION AND ITS POTENTIAL TO EMPOWER EVERY STUDENT TO REALIZE THEIR RIGHT TO ACCESS INFORMATION. ■ LIBRARIES HELP EDUCATE PEOPLE TO MAKE INFORMED DECISIONS. ■ LIBRARIANS ARE PRIMARY GUIDES TO INFORMATION RESOURCES AND FACILITATORS FOR THEIR USE. ■ THE EXPONENTIAL GROWTH IN INFORMATION UNDERSCORES THE IMPORTANCE OF THE USE OF TECHNOLOGICAL ADVANCES IN ADDRESSING PATRONS' NEEDS. ■ ALTHOUGH OPPORTUNE USE OF NEW TECHNOLOGIES IS A KEY MECHANISM FOR IMPROVING INFORMATION ACCESS, KNOWLEDGEABLE AND ENTHUSIASTIC LIBRARY STAFF IS ESSENTIAL TO TIMELY AND ACCURATE INFORMATION RETRIEVAL.

Statements taken from "The Guiding Principles for Illinois Libraries" issued by the Illinois State Library, Spring 1994, and "A Draft Proposal for Graduation From Augustana", September 5, 1990.

MISSION OF THE ABELL LIBRARY

The mission of the Abell Library is to support the "Mission of Austin College."
Towards this end, the Library fulfills its mission by the provision of recorded
expression and knowledge through 1) on-site provision of print, electronic, and
other formats; and 2) access to off-site resources both through traditional services,
such as interlibrary loan, and links to electronic databases to the degree possible
within human and economic limitations and the needs of the Austin College
community. To adequately fulfill its mission, the Abell Library must go beyond
its responsibilities of acquiring, organizing, and making available recorded
materials. It must seek actively, through collaboration with the classroom faculty,
to facilitate the interaction between users of recorded materials to develop those
skills necessary to acquire and evaluate critically the information available in the
various formats. Finally, the Abell Library fulfills its mission through the
provision of facilities for the convenient storage, retrieval, and use of recorded
materials in whatever form may be required by the curriculum and, to the degree
possible, the other needs and interests of the Austin College community. The
Abell Library provides the appropriate environment for users to engage in a
variety of learning activities supporting the mission of Austin College.

Approved by the Library Advisory Committee
November 26, 1996

GOALS OF THE ABELL LIBRARY

I. Services to the Academic Community and General Public

A. Provide efficient and courteous assistance to all library patrons

B. Provide access to library collections through policies and hours of service that reflect the needs of the Austin College Community

C. Teach students the skills necessary to locate, evaluate, and use recorded knowledge effectively in its many formats, with a view towards the development of independent, lifelong reamers.

D. Collaborate with the classroom faculty in the development of instructional programs that enable students to use the Abell Library and other libraries effectively.

E. Establish and maintain a dialogue with the Austin College community to both understand the community's needs and to keep the community informed of the Abell Library's policies, programs, and services.

F. Foster cultural awareness and appreciation of the book and other library materials through library exhibits, collections, and programs.

II. On-Site Collections

A. Identify, with the active participation of the classroom faculty, those materials that:
   1. Support present and anticipated curricula
   2. Are necessary to develop and maintain outstanding undergraduate collections in subject fields emphasized at Austin College
   3. Are necessary to develop and maintain a general library collection suited to the needs and interests of the Austin College community.

   Note: The scope and breadth of the collection should reflect the needs it serves (See Collection Development Policy).

B. Develop and maintain appropriate procedures for the acceptance and maintenance of materials donated to Austin College and the Abell Library.

C. Maintain on-site collections in an easily accessible, logical, and orderly arrangement that conforms to accepted standards and meets the needs of users of the Abell Library.

D. Provide for the availability and use of the on-site collections in a manner consistent with the Abell Library's responsibility to protect and preserve the collection for future use.

E. Respect legal restrictions on use of library materials.

F. Circulate materials according to policies and guidelines that reflect the needs of the Austin College community.

III. Information Access from Off-Site Sources

A. Cooperate with libraries, vendors, and others to maximize access to sources of information not owned by Austin College and housed in the Abell Library.

B. Respect legal restrictions on the use of borrowed and electronically accessible materials.

IV. Resources of the Library

A. Human Resources of the Abell Library

1. Attract, develop, and retain the best qualified staff possible.
2. Provide opportunities and incentives for professional development for all library staff.
3. Appropriately define the library positions.
4. Document clearly the expectations and performance of all library employees using a fair and efficient method.
5. Encourage high staff productivity and morale.

B. Facilities

    1. Provide space, equipment, and technology to support the mission of the Abell Library and Austin College.
    2. Provide facilities conducive to study and intellectual exchange.
    3. Provide safe, clean facilities necessary for a positive work environment.
    4. Provide access to all members of the Austin College community regardless of physical ability.

C. Finances

    1. Manage the finances of the library according to both established principles of library management and Austin College policy, so as to optimize available resources.
    2. Achieve and/or maintain a level of financial support comparable to that of other liberal arts colleges of the first rank.
    3. Monitor on-going issues related to cost of library resources.

V. Administration

A. Promote the fulfillment of the "Mission of Abell Library" and the achievement of the "Goals of the Abell Library."

B. Promote cooperation and communication within and among all departments of the Abell Library.

C. Promote constructive relationships with the College's administration, academic departments, students, and the Abell Library's public in general.

D. Assess regularly and systematically the activities, programs, departments, and staff of Abell Library.

E. Coordinate the programs and resources of the Abell Library.

G. Plan, develop, and articulate strategies for the improvement of the Abell Library in its support of the Mission of Austin College.

VI. Evaluation

A. Seek feedback from the service community as part of an ongoing effort to evaluate the success with which the Abell Library achieves its goals and fulfills its mission.

B. Improve existing programs and implement new programs based on the feedback and evaluation.

C. Review regularly the mission and goals of the Abell Library.

VII. Future

A. Plan and develop strategies for enhancing the programs and resources of the Abell Library to support the anticipated library-related needs of the Austin College community.

B. Monitor new trends and technologies in information access and delivery and keep members of the Austin College community informed of them.

C. Plan for the future in light of ongoing changes in technology, capital improvement plans, and educational pedagogy.

Approved by the Library Advisory
Committee February 6, 1997
goalsc.doc
LLH

Bates College
The George and Helen Ladd Library
Lewiston, ME 04240

Mission Statement of Ladd Library

"As a college of the liberal arts and sciences, Bates offers a
curriculum and faculty that challenge students to attain intellectual
achievements and to develop powers of critical assessment, analysis,
expression, aesthetic sensibility, and independent thought.
       The College expects students to appreciate the discoveries and
insights of established traditions of learners, as well as to participate in the
resolution of what is unknown."

Bates College Institutional Mission statement, 1995.

The Library at Bates exists to further the academic mission of the College
by developing collections and offering services which focus upon the
curriculum needs of undergraduate students, which further their research
and scholarly needs, and which provide general knowledge for their
current interests and their continuing education.

The Library provides, and expects its users to maintain, an atmosphere in
which study and research can take place in a variety of comfortable
environments appropriate to individual and group learning and instruction.
The expert staff serves to enable easy access to information in many
formats and to instruct in the use of information resources. It is the
Library's goal to foster an awareness and appreciation of the intellectual
and aesthetic pleasure and value to be had in reading, research, and the
gathering of information.

Where possible within its resources, and when consistent with its primary
responsibilities to undergraduate students, the Library extends services to
others in the Bates community, the wider geographical area, and the
library profession.

LIBRARY VISION

The vision of the Corriher-Linn-Black Library is to be an excellent college and community resource, preparing students for graduate-level study and careers of their choosing, and providing intellectual enrichment for the campus and Salisbury/Rowan County communities.

LIBRARY MISSION

The Corriher-Linn-Black Library serves as an active agent to enable its users to become self-directed, lifelong learners. The Library, as the information hub for the College and a community resource, provides a diverse population of students, faculty, staff, and community borrowers onsite and electronic access to information resources in a variety of formats on campus, in the Salisbury/Rowan community, and throughout the nation and the world.

Library services support and enrich academic curricula, programs, and activities, while providing Catawba students with opportunities for individual growth and development within the context of a liberal education. The Library introduces students to the library research process by offering instruction in traditional research methods and by providing hands-on experience with emerging information technologies.

Library Mission rewritten and approved 4/98
Library Vision written and approved 4/98

D'Youville College

Mission of the Library

The library's mission is to actively participate in the education of students, and to support the informational needs of the entire College community. This community includes students, faculty, administration, support staff, alumni, and the high school students and faculty that are affiliated with the college.

The college provides education at the baccalaureate and masters levels emphasizing teaching, and encourages scholarship and lifelong learning. Its primary focus is the application of knowledge in the liberal arts, science, business, education, health, and human services. The library will provide the resources and services required to foster academic excellence and freedom of inquiry in these areas of study. This mission can only be fulfilled if there is complete utilization of library resources. Effective utilization is dependent on interaction between faculty, administration, and library staff. Therefore, the librarians, working with other faculty, will promote an information literacy program to meet the needs of various disciplines. As the college grows, the library will be flexible and open to new ideas so that as different formats or programs become a reality, the library will continue to provide quality service. Directives and guidelines from the federal and state governments, and the accrediting associations for higher education programs will be applied to the library strategic plan assuring that the library achieves its mission.

Vision of the Library

D'Youville College is a complex and changing educational enterprise predicated on a strong liberal arts foundation, emphasizing broadly based core requirements for all undergraduate programs. Among the programs making heaviest demands on the library are the rehabilitation and health sciences, and education, professions which require state of the art scholarship and research. Writing a thesis is requisite to graduation for approximately 50 percent of the students including all occupational and physical therapy, dietetics, graduate nursing, health services administration, and special education students.

The library is an essential support to all of D'Youville's academic programs and must be a prominent symbol of the College's commitment to the excellence of those programs. The central focus of the library is the information contained in its collection which is the hub of the teaching and learning environment. It is the foundation for the intellectual life of the faculty, staff, and students. Accessibility to the collection must be assured through appropriate staffing, equipment, and automation.

The Library Resource Center's support of academic programs shall extend to creating a comfortable and inviting atmosphere. Such support would be manifest in a variety of study and support facilities, including handicap accessibility. In addition to adequate seating configured in several ways, there should be group study rooms and special study rooms equipped with instrumentation and furniture appropriate to the programs offered at the College.

Finally, the library must be a central pillar supporting an effective learning environment for D'Youville's students and programs. It should have the capacity to display materials and artifacts, have sufficient gathering spaces for students and faculty, and contain a large flexible space which can support multimedia presentations. As the center of the intellectual life of the College, consideration must be given to its connectedness to other campus buildings and the security of its staff, equipment, and collections.

Earlham College Libraries
Richmond, Indiana

Mission statement

The Earlham College libraries support the mission of the College by providing access to information resources and facilitating their use.

Goals

This mission is forwarded through programs and activities which strive to achieve the following goals:

(1)   Develop a collection (e.g. print, microforms, electronic) information resources that meet the information needs of the students, faculty and staff of the college as they engage in the teaching/learning process.

(2)   Provide methods for accessing information resources owned by us or maintained by other information providers.

(3)   Provide a program of course-integrated instruction and reference services that will help prepare students to be effective life-long learners.

(4)   Provide a collection of materials and supporting services for the study of the Society of Friends, particularly in the Midwest.

(5)   Provide a library facility with physical environment and ambient that is conducive to the use and preservation of information resources. and which promotes the use of information resources.

(6)   Provide efficient and effective internal processes to enhance services.

(7)   Develop closer working relationships with Computer Services and Media Resources units to work towards an integrated information services program for the College community.

(8)   Provide staff development opportunities that will stimulate thinking about the improvement of library services and prepare staff to become effective in improving those services.

(9)   Maintain awareness of new developments in librarianship, information management, and services.

Approved September, 1995 by Library Staff

EAST TEXAS BAPTIST UNIVERSITY
Marshall, Texas

University Library Mission Statement

The Mamye Jarrett Learning Center (the University Library) supports the mission of the University through its collections, services, staff, and study facilities.

In building the collection, the Library seeks to acquire resources that give students not only a broad view of the humanities, natural and social sciences, and fine arts, but also a comprehensive treatment of areas in which majors and minors are offered at the undergraduate and graduate levels. Consistent with the University's intention to develop graduates with intellectual inquiry, social consciousness, and Christian character, the Library also seeks to provide information on the current state of the nation and the world and recreational interests of students.

Through its service programs--reference service, orientation activities, bibliographic instruction, interlibrary loan, electronic delivery of information--the Library exercises a teaching role designed to assist students in developing the critical knowledge of resources, libraries, bibliographic organization, and information technology that can lead to lifelong learning.

The Library seeks to recruit and/or develop a staff with sympathy for students, an understanding of the educational process, and a dedication to Christian liberal arts education. In addition to knowledge of information sources and library organization, professional library staff members need the ability to interact smoothly with students and faculty in promoting effective use of information resources for instructional purposes.

The Library seeks to provide an inviting, convenient place for study and for use of library materials. Convenient library hours, adequate environmental control, sufficient study spaces, comfortable seating, and properly-functioning equipment are all necessary for the fullest possible use of library materials.

Adopted by the Library Staff, August 1987.
Reviewed and reaffirmed, October 1992.
Revised and reaffirmed, October 1996.

PURPOSE

In keeping with the goals of Christian higher education and the purpose of Gardner-Webb University, it is the mission of Dover Memorial Library to advance the academic and general endeavors of the Gardner-Webb community, meeting current informational needs and fostering the development of individuals committed to lifelong learning.

GOALS AND OBJECTIVES

The Library seeks to take an active role in the teaching process by:

Providing ample, accessible resources, in a variety of formats, to support the curriculum.

Providing a competent, service-oriented professional and support staff who relish the role of facilitator --- connecting students, faculty, and other patrons with the resources they need, and fostering critical inquiry.

Providing both teaching and non-teaching services which advance the instructional program.

Providing a comfortable, efficient library facility with appropriate technology, both traditional and innovative, for enhanced service to its patrons.

The Library seeks to further the development of the student as a member of the global community and a lifelong learner by:

Providing resources which reflect a variety of viewpoints and philosophies, and reflect a broad spectrum of ideas.

Providing resources which are appropriate for personal growth and development, and those which support the curriculum.

Encouraging open inquiry, intellectual integrity, and the development of critical thinking.

The Library seeks to meet its responsibility to the larger community by :

Welcoming all responsible patrons to the Library, and encouraging them to make use of our resources.

Providing assistance to all patrons in the use of our materials and equipment.

Providing the opportunity for individuals to participate in the community borrower program.

FOLKE BERNADOTTE MEMORIAL LIBRARY
GUSTAVUS ADOLPHUS COLLEGE
MISSION AND STATEMENT OF GOALS

Folke Bernadotte Memorial Library develops and promotes access to library resources in support of the mission of Gustavus Adolphus College. The Library provides resources and information services to meet the needs of undergraduate curricula and research, administrative support, and the intellectual life of the college and wide community. As multimedia, electronic and network technologies evolve, the Library will participate actively in their development and integration for campus-wide information access. Through instruction in the use, interpretation, and evaluation of information resources, the staff advances the teaching mission of the Library and the College. The Library endeavors to create and sustain a learning environment that promotes respect, fairness, diversity, and intellectual growth and excellence.

STATEMENT OF GOALS

I. Develop strong information and research resources:

1. Select and acquire resources appropriate to support the liberal arts curriculum and to enrich the intellectual environment of the College and greater community through collection development in collaboration with faculty.

2. Organize and manage collections and other information resources, regardless of format, by providing appropriate forms of bibliographic access and working toward integration of traditional and non-traditional formats.

3. Promote the preservation and conservation of library materials to ensure the availability of the collection for future users.

4. Continue development and utilization of specialized collections that are distinctive to Gustavus Adolphus College and are of national, historic or scholarly interest

5. Participate in resource sharing and other cooperative efforts to enhance access to information and to further the development and use of local resources.

II. Provide effective library services:

1. Provide instructional and reference services covering all information resources and processes, thereby fostering a collaborative learning environment for the Library's constituencies.

2. Facilitate access to information at Gustavus Adolphus College and elsewhere through services including on-site use, online catalog, circulation, course reserves, maintenance of the stacks, interlibrary loan, and various kinds of electronic services.

3. Provide a range of services through a well-staffed library, an audio-visual department, a selective depository of federal government documents, a special collection of rare books, the college and church Archives, and the Lund Music Library.

4. Promote awareness, understanding and use of the Folke Bernadotte Memorial Library through orientation sessions, ongoing user education, publications, exhibits, outreach, and other kinds of publicity.

III. Build and maintain an appropriate technological and physical environment:

1. Monitor developments in computing, physical networking and information technology, implementing appropriate technologies to enhance the quality and cost-effectiveness of library staff operations and patron services.

2. Work closely with services both on and off campus which provide use of computing, communications, media and other support to achieve integrated and effective mechanisms for access to information resources at the campus, state, regional and national level.

3. Maintain the physical facilities and equipment necessary for the proper utilization, processing, storage and preservation of library materials in all formats, and for the continued provision of appropriate information services.

4. Provide an attractive, healthful and safe environment for work and study.

5. Strive for access to library facilities and services by all patrons and staff.

IV. Manage a responsive and responsible workplace:

1. Organize and administer library operations through effective planning, evaluation, and budgeting.

2. Promote the recruitment and development of a qualified and motivated staff by providing resources for training, staff development and continuing education; by encouraging participation in professional, paraprofessional and college activities.

3. Provide a supportive working environment for student library assistants.

4. Support communication, participation, and innovation through formal and informal opportunities and flexible organizational structures.

5. Adhere to recognized library, academic, and workplace standards that address technical, operation, service, safety, legal and ethical issues.

2/10/94

Mission Statement for Duggan Library

The Duggan Library is a locus for scholarly activity, in which students, faculty, and librarians work together in the venture of learning, and is also a seat of intellectual endeavor for our community. Committed to the unfettered pursuit of knowledge, the Library vigorously and visibly sustains the academic mission of Hanover College.

Librarians, students, and faculty work closely together to:

ensure that the Library collects, and acts as a gateway for, materials that inspire intellectual vitality and support the scholarly activity at Hanover College;

make the best use of information resources in all formats.

The Librarians:

engage the community in information literacy initiatives, including teaching how information is organized and how to conduct research;

periodically evaluate the library facilities, programs, policies, materials, and services to ensure that the intellectual and scholarly needs of the Hanover College community are being met:

seek and maintain cooperative alliances to complement the resources available locally.

Library Vision Statement

Illinois Wesleyan University

Bloomington, IL

The vision of the Illinois Wesleyan University Library is a learning environment responding to the traditional values of a liberal arts university and to current technological advances, integrating technology within tradition. As the intellectual heart of the campus, the library is the locus where scholarly information, regardless of format, is gathered, organized, and prepared for dissemination to the University community. In addition, the library provides a place for interaction, collaboration, consultation, study and reflection.

Driven by feedback from the campus community, those involved in the planning process envision a structure that is both externally majestic and internally inviting, reflecting the traditional heritage of an academic undergraduate library. On the entry level, library exhibits, new books and periodicals, newspapers, and a specially appointed public reading area will welcome library users. Books will be in full view on all levels, with contiguous, quiet reading spaces that take full advantage of abundant natural lighting. A culture of reflective scholarship will be eloquently, captured in the contemplative atmosphere of the University Archives and Special Collections reading room. The new library will also incorporate the substantial collections of an existing, branch music library, making these resources more readily available to the wider university community. Particular attention will be given to a combined Media/Listening Center, bringing together audio/visual materials from various disciplines, while providing close proximity to subject-related print and electronic resources. Important to note is the design accommodation and administrative support for aggressive growth of the print resources collection: the library book collection, as an example, will double within the next ten years.

With careful consideration of the circumstances and environment in which a library researcher (whether faculty, student, or member of the larger University community) approaches and uses information resources, the decision was made to organize information by intellectual content rather than separating resources into collections by physical format. This process of integrating information resources is already taking shape with the library's use of the campus local area network. The library links electronic information resources, whether accessible through subscription, contract, or publicly available on the Internet, through coordinated, subject-based webpages. To further this process within the new library, the periodical collection will be integrated into the book stacks so that journals and monographs in a discipline will be located together. Networked computer workstations will be dispersed throughout the stack areas as well, allowing electronic resources to be used in conjunction with print resources. Viewed as an extension of the collection, these workstations will enable the researcher to gather, analyze, and assimilate the accessible knowledge of a particular field of study. In this way, the library envisions the merging of traditional research methodology with the advantages of state-of-the-art information technology.

Acknowledging that familiarity and understanding of library tools and technology are on a continuum from novice to expert, detailed design consideration has been given to research needs at each stage of inquiry and ability, especially in the Information Commons. The Information Commons consists of multiple users, networked workstations, the print reference collection, group project rooms for collaborative work, and an adjacent instruction lab. The networked lab will serve as the appropriate space for formal, hands-on, interactive instruction of library print and electronic resources. When an instruction class is not scheduled, the lab will be available for general use. The entire Information Commons area benefits from close proximity to expert staff at the service desk. Beyond the Information Commons, the variety, number, and proportion of styles of seating is in direct response to faculty and student input. Solitary researchers will enjoy comfortable, private, reading chairs and carrels, capable of accepting computer technology. A large number of networked group study rooms responds to the campus pedagogical trend of student work in groups. Ubiquitous wiring assures that the new building is as technologically flexible as possible, providing a variety of captivating atmospheres to utilize electronic access.

Technology within tradition: Illinois Wesleyan University's library vision integrates the rich network of digital resources with the culture of traditions academic scholarship. With inviting spaces for both individuals and groups, the new library will serve as both the gateway to campus and as the gateway to the breadth of resources and materials that bridges information into knowledge.

October 1996

Lightner Library at Keuka College
Vision, mission and goals statement
1997-1998

Vision: To be the gateway to information and the center for training users to
            successfully use and access information

Mission: Provide access to electronic and paper resources which support the curriculum of
            Keuka College, provide ongoing educational opportunities for learning to
            effectively access and evaluate information, and create an environment which
            facilitates learning

LYNCHBURG COLLEGE LIBRARY

MISSION STATEMENT

The library supports learning
by providing information services
to meet the needs of students and faculty.

VISION STATEMENT

The library will serve as a conduit to discovery and self-education by:
♦ focussing on users' needs
♦ enabling users to become information literate
♦ acquiring and organizing information resources
♦ acting as a guide to information utilizing traditional formats and innovative technology.

MISSION STATEMENT

Mabee Library and Learning Resource Center provides a comprehensive program of library services for the students, faculty, and staff of MidAmerica Nazarene University. By being the instructional materials center of the university, the Library provides books, periodicals, and computerized resources to implement the curriculum and to foster cultural appreciation. The staff promotes and encourages patrons to develop library skills that will facilitate life-long learning. Mabee Library provides resources for patrons in the most efficient way while maintaining set policies and procedures. The Library gives support to the patron in his pursuit of academic, vocational, general understanding, and cultural goals. The privileges of the Library are also available in a limited way to community area patrons.

Dr. Ray L. Morrison
Library Director

http://www.mnu.edu/ibrary/mission.html

MIDDLEBURY COLLEGE

THE MISSION OF THE LIBRARY

The mission of the Middlebury College Library is to promote the ability to seek, evaluate, and employ library resources in the full exercise of freedom of inquiry which is an integral part of the education of students in the liberal arts and sciences. To this end, the Library develops collections which uphold the learning and teaching objectives of a strong undergraduate institution; organizes and provides both intellectual and physical access to materials; and guides members of our academic community toward a grasp of bibliographic and technical skills which facilitate use of the collections at hand and information resources worldwide.

GOALS OF THE LIBRARY

TO SERVE OUR ACADEMIC COMMUNITY:

- By teaching students to seek, evaluate, and use information in their studies at Middlebury and in preparation for their work in the world.

- By working with faculty to meet student needs for bibliographic instruction.

- By providing faculty and other staff with resources they need to fulfill their educational mission.

- By implementing policies and procedures which encourage full and responsible use of the Library's resources and services by all who use it.

- By developing links to other libraries, collections, organizations, and networks in order to expand the resources available to library users.

TO DEVELOP, ORGANIZE, AND MAINTAIN COLLECTIONS:

- By acquiring materials as described in our collection development policies with subject emphases in accord with the curriculum.

- By organizing the collections and providing full bibliographic and physical access to materials.

- By developing and maintaining databases and information management systems that provide effective and efficient access to library materials and resources of interest to our academic community.

- By maintaining the collections as responsible stewards using proven preservation techniques.

- By building upon established special collections which preserve for future generations library and archival materials important to Middlebury College.

TO ADMINISTER RESOURCES EFFECTIVELY:

- By ensuring that facilities are adequate to house and service the collections; that space and environment allow both users and staff to work productively; and that equipment and systems used to carry out the programs of the Library are equal to the tasks we need to accomplish.

- By reviewing and evaluating, on a regular basis, our mission and goals, policies, programs, personnel, equipment, systems, and facilities in order to improve effectiveness in accomplishing our mission.

  - By recognizing that our success depends upon human resources and implementing policies which foster staff development.

  - By establishing a dialogue with all segments of the College community which promotes understanding of Library policies, programs and needs, and facilitates our awareness of developments which have implications for the Library.

  - By actively planning for the future role of the Library in the life of the College in light of technical developments in the storage and transfer of information, capital improvement plans, and changes in the College's educational program.

GUIDING PRINCIPLES

We are guided by principles outlined in the Library Bill of Rights:*

1. *Books and other library resources should be provided for the interests, information, and enlightenment of all people of the community the library serves. Materials should not be excluded because of the origin, background, or views of those contributing to their creation.*

2. *Libraries should provide materials and information presenting all points of view on current and historical issues. Materials should not be proscribed or removed because of partisan or doctrinal disapproval.*

3. *Libraries should challenge censorship in the fulfillment of their responsibility to provide information and enlightenment.*

4. *Libraries should cooperate with all persons and groups concerned with resisting abridgment of free expression and free access to ideas.*

5. *A person's right to use a library should not be denied or abridged because of origin, age, background, or views.*

In endorsing these statements we seek to guard against incursions upon the academic freedom of the teacher in teaching and the rights of the student in learning.

*adopted June 18, 1948, amended February 2, 1961, June 27, 1967, and January 23, 1980, by the American Library Association.

June 1990

Mt. St. Mary College

MISSION STATEMENT

The mission of the Curtin Memorial Library is to acquire, organize, and disseminate recorded information which supports the educational programs and research efforts of the college community and which prepares students to function responsibly as individuals within an ever changing society.

In keeping with this mission statement it is the responsibility of the library to strive toward the following goals:

Goal 1: To provide and maintain bibliographic, electronic and human resources which support the academic programs and research needs of all library users by:

  1. Acquiring and organizing recorded information regardless of physical format.

  2. Furnishing a balanced collection of library materials which support classroom instruction and student research.

  3. Adopting appropriate technology for information storage and retrieval.

  4. Ensuring an adequate library facility which encourages optimal library use.

  5. Providing professional and support staff adequate to meet student and faculty demand for information.

Goal 2: To teach students and other library users information literacy and the skills needed to access recorded information by:

  1. Providing interpretive services (bibliographic instruction, reference, database searching, etc...) to assist student and faculty researchers in using the collection.

  2. Reinforcing the institutional role of reference services through workshops and seminars.

  3. Continuing to explore and implement new methods of library literacy instruction.

Goal 3: To view the library as a dynamic system requiring continuous evaluation by:

  1. Constantly working to achieve recognized library standards.

  2. Seeking improved methods of delivering information in a timely manner.

5/96

C. GOALS AND MEANS STATEMENTS OF THE ACADEMIC-SUPPORT AREAS.

1. THE MOUNT UNION COLLEGE LIBRARY

The Mount Union College Library provides information resources and services designed to promote a wide range of learning experiences. Library staff play an important role in the teaching of the research skills needed for academic success and for life in an information society and seek to accomplish this through:

- Providing instruction in the use of library resources, with an emphasis on the informed evaluation of research results, encouraging users to develop the skills to be successful in an information rich environment;

  - Work with mentors in the preparation of library instruction for incoming freshmen, including the library portion of the LS 100 textbook.

  - Develop library usage aids offered through the campus home page.

  - Prepare lectures providing library instruction for both general and specialized classes.

  - Teach a college credit course in research and information literacy.

  - Provide reference assistance and instruction in the use of information sources, both print and electronic, tailored to the needs of the specific user.

  - Select reference sources, both print and electronic, which are user-friendly and compliment our other collections.

  - Provide assistance in the use of mechanical and automated library equipment.

  - Instruct Computer Center Help Desk staff to assist users in accessing library electronic resources.

- Developing excellent campus collections and providing access to external resources which support the College curriculum and promote the study of all cultures;

  - Work with faculty to build collections, both print and electronic, which support the college curriculum.

  - Select additional materials which enhance campus life and promote cultural literacy.

  - Evaluate and weed existing collections, identifying areas which need to be strengthened.

  - Provide full descriptive cataloging for all library acquisitions.

  - Establish authority control procedures for the enrichment of library database access points.

  - Catalog departmental and other campus collections making them accessible through the library system.

  - Provide campus-wide network access to the library catalog and library net-based reference and full-text sources.

- Provide fully automated Circulation and Reserve services.

- Provide Interlibrary Loan service for the retrieval of materials from other libraries.

- Join the OhioLink project, with a consortium of other libraries, giving our users access to all OhioLink resources.

- Participate in state and local cooperatives providing access to OhioLink and other regional libraries.

- Provide community access to our library collections, including government documents.

- Creating a comfortable atmosphere suitable for the use of information resources in all formats and designed to support a wide array of study and research activities;

  - Provide both public hours and service staffing designed to match the usage patterns of our patrons.

  - Maintain specialized library collections in subject areas where the demand levels or specialized needs are justified (Cope and Wilson Hall Libraries).

  - Renovate existing library facilities and plan the library components of the proposed Information Services Center.

  - Develop a total of 400 study seats, with at least 100 in group study arrangements, in the new and existing buildings.

  - Provide adequate lighting for the efficient retrieval and use of library materials.

  - Plan all new facilities to meet ADA handicapped access requirements

  - Provide and maintain all equipment needed for the efficient use of library resources.

  - Work with Computer Center staff to provide the technology needed for the effective use of library resources campus-wide.

  - Work with campus security staff to provide a secure environment for both users and collections.

- Encouraging the continued professional development of library staff as effective intermediaries in a rapidly changing environment.

  - Purchase and maintain a collection of materials in the field of library science for the continuing educational use of library staff.

  - Subsidize membership in professional societies whose activities enhance professional growth.

  - Encourage library staff to attend professional meetings sponsored by national and regional library organizations.

- Encourage staff to take part in training offered by consortiums and vendors.

- Implement a program of internal training in which staff members share their expertise.

- Encourage library personnel to consult with the staff of other libraries in order to compare methods.

- Implement a formal training program for student assistants.

- Promote cooperation with other information services groups on campus.

- Create job descriptions for all library positions and improve the employee evaluation process.

Ohio Wesleyan University

STATEMENT ON OHIO WESLEYAN UNIVERSITY LIBRARY

The role of the Ohio Wesleyan University Library system is to participate actively in the instructional process as a "teaching library". A "teaching library" is a library which is integrally and directly involved in implementing the University Statement of Aims, in addition to serving as a support service for academic programs. The library system carries out the role of "teaching library" by:

(a) encouraging and facilitating life-long learning through the development of instructional programs which emphasize investigative skills;

(b) providing distinctive programs and services designed to meet the intellectual and cultural needs of our students, faculty, staff, alumni and community; and

(c) developing an organized collection of materials and equipment and establishing information services which best satisfy the present and future needs of the university relating to teaching, research, and community service.

The Ohio Wesleyan University library system refers to Beeghly Library, the Audio-Visual Center, and all branch libraries.

RATIONALE

The University prides itself on its Statement of Aims and each academic department lists, in the Catalogue, a statement of its relationship to the University's educational mission. Currently, there is no written policy linking the library system with that mission. Because of its functions and relationship to education at Ohio Wesleyan, the Library system should have a mission statement emphasizing this relationship. It is the belief of the Committee on Teaching and Learning that this mission statement will provide a basis for the development of suitable operating policies.

Accepted for adoption by the faculty on April 15, 1985

I. Purpose of the McGraw-Page Library

In support of the mission of Randolph-Macon College, the library facilitates the use of information and learning resources by students, faculty, and staff. As an integral part of the teaching/learning process, the library supports the scholarship, research, artistic endeavors, and other intellectual explorations of students, faculty, and staff.

The library maintains strong, up-to-date undergraduate collections in various formats, offers a broad range of library services, and provides ready access to its own collections and to those of outside libraries, external databases, and other information resources. The McGraw-Page Library facility provides an inviting environment conducive to study and research.

Librarians give reference assistance and provide instruction in the use of information resources. They work cooperatively with other faculty in helping students improve their skills in finding needed information and in evaluating sources.

Library Document
5/11/98
Page No. 2

MISSION STATEMENT OF LAVERY LIBRARY

To: — Serve library patrons by acquiring, or providing access to, information sources that support their curricular and other informational needs.

— Organize, preserve and update information sources for maximum accessibility.

— Teach library patrons to select, evaluate, and use, information

In A Way That: — Treats everyone with warmth, courtesy, and respect, conveying a strong sense of personal service.

— Collaborates with faculty and students in the teaching and learning processes.

— Anticipates and adjusts to the changing conditions of patrons, the college, and the environment.

— Utilizes available funds in an efficient and appropriate manner.

— Provides an environment that encourages professional growth.

So That: — Patrons have their information needs met efficiently.

— Patrons acquire the skills necessary to be literate in the increasingly complex arena of information searching, thereby giving them tools for lifelong learning.

— The Mission of Saint John Fisher College is supported and enhanced.

MISSION STATEMENT

The mission of Spring Hill College is the formation of men and women into persons who are intellectually, spiritually, socially and morally mature. The purpose of the library is to support that mission.

In particular, the library strives to meet American Library Association standards for academic library facilities, staff, resources and services, recognizing that standards are a means to an end. That end is to create an environment that

1) encourages users to ask for assistance
2) provides information on available resources and services
3) introduces users to new information technologies
4) provides resources adequate to support curricular needs
5) fosters independent thinking
6) assures users acquire a broad understanding of information skills and sources and become "information literate"

The library must provide an atmosphere that promotes study, encourages scholarly pursuits, and fosters the academic excellence that is the primary goal of the College. It does this by maintaining physical space where individuals and small groups can comfortably engage in formal scholarly activities or in the serendipitous pursuit of knowledge that a good library will engender. Space must also be provided, along with necessary furnishings and equipment, for the convenient storage, retrieval, and use of recorded knowledge in whatever form may be required by the curriculum, and to the degree feasible, by the research and other interests of the community.

It is the responsibility of the library to maintain a quality collection of materials that furthers the purpose and mission of the institution as a whole in meeting the needs of students. The primary emphasis should be on those materials likely to be used by faculty in preparing their courses and by students in doing research related to their studies. Faculty scholarship in the College is, of course, essential, and it is a secondary mission of the library to facilitate this by providing the basic materials faculty need to carry on research to the degree possible within the limited resources available.

However, the intensive collecting of materials that are unlikely to be used by students in order to support faculty research or the building of highly specialized resources to support advanced studies that will never be part of the Spring Hill curriculum are outside the scope of the library program at Spring Hill.

The library must provide services to its users that are designed to facilitate the identification, location, delivery and use of recorded knowledge. If the curriculum determines the focus of the library, then these services need to be integrated into the teaching and research fiber of the College. This can be accomplished only through an active and continuing dialogue among faculty, library staff, and students that has as its goal the development of maximum facility in the use of recorded knowledge by students. Moreover, the library works to integrate library instruction with classroom instruction and to devise staged and continuing programs that reinforce basic and advanced information skills.

In addition to direct- support of curricular and student and faculty information and research needs, the library attempts to create a balanced collection, to introduce new information technologies and to make materials and technologies available in such a way as to create an environment that challenges students to develop basic information skills that they can carry with them through the workplace, advanced education and lifelong learning.

The degree to which the library fulfills its mission can be measured by the degree to which it (1) meets recognized standards for facilities, budget, resources, staff and services, (2) supports the College's mission by acquiring and teaching the use of resources relevant to the curriculum and (3) provides an information environment that challenges and cultivates independent thinking and information literacy.

3/9/89

TRANSYLVANIA UNIVERSITY

STATEMENT OF LIBRARY MISSION

The principal mission of the library is to provide information resources and services in support of Transylvania University's mission of liberal education. Centering on the free search for knowledge and understanding, the college strives to educate youth for responsible citizenship, meaningful careers, lifelong learning, and a humane existence.

To accomplish its mission of support, the library acquires, organizes, manages, and preserves appropriate materials for the instructional and general intellectual needs of the institution. Furthermore, the library staff, working with the faculty, develops learning skills and encourages the effective utilization of library resources through assistance and instruction in the organization and use of libraries, electronic information resources, and the bibliographies of various disciplines.

An additional mission of the library is to acquire, organize, manage and preserve appropriate materials for Special Collections and the archives of Transylvania, especially--but not limited to--those relating to the history of Transylvania and to the role of the institution in the Commonwealth of Kentucky.

Adopted October 1993

Trinity College of Vermont

Trinity College of Vermont Library

Last updated 07/06/98

Primary Activities of Library

➡ Support the College's instructional and research programs through ownership of, or access to, appropriate print and computerized resources.

➡ Provide assistance to the Library's users in their search for useful information resources, to the end of furthering their self-sufficiency in this or any other library.

➡ Provide a comfortable study and learning environment for the Library's users.

Strengths of the Library

➡ The Library is open 97.5 hours/week during the academic year, including evenings and weekends, with full service available from permanent staff during all those hours.

➡ All of the Library's owned books, journals, microfilms, videos and other materials are catalogued in a computerized system which is available on multiple work stations throughout the Library, on the College's campus network, and, through the Internet, world-wide.

➡ The Library's users consistently praise the availability and excellence of services they receive from the Library's staff.

➡ The Library is able to fill its users' needs for specific materials almost 100% of the time, either through its owned resources or through collaborative arrangements with other academic libraries.

➡ The Library has consistently obtained timely new information resources for the College's new programs, including for the Master's level programs in Criminal Justice and Community Mental Health.

➡ The Library provides an extensive Internet web page which has the dual purpose of enhancing the Library's services on-campus and extending those services further off-campus.

➡ The Library's staff is uniformly dedicated to providing the most supportive and useful service to all of the Library's users, both directly and behind the scenes.

➡ The Library building (dedicated in 1985) and its appointments are attractive and functional.

Continuing Goals

➡ Assure that the Library serves all students, faculty and programs by enhancing access and expanding collections including electronic formats.

➡ Assure that the Library's computer resource developments parallel those of the College, with functional interactivity between the two.

➡ Respond to library service and collection implications of a more diverse student body, including international students.

➡ Identify and address differing library service approaches demanded by graduate education.

➡ Develop appropriate support for any future new or changed programs and directions of the College, as these become known.

➡ Define and address library needs for off-campus students.

➡ Define and expand site-specific library support for programs primarily offered as distance education.

➡ Further develop provisions for library services through electronic and cooperative arrangements as needed.

---

http://www.trinityvt.edu/alib/libgoals.htm

MISSION STATEMENT AND GOALS

MISSION STATEMENT

The primary mission of the University Library is to provide the members of the academic community access to resources that support the current and anticipated instructional, research, and service programs of the University of the South, as well as to promote understanding of effective ways to use these resources. In addition, the library contributes to the culture and informational resources of the surrounding community. The University Library also serves as a Federal Government Depository.

GOALS

A. Services: To provide accurate, efficient, and courteous assistance to users in identifying, locating, and using the information resources they need.

1. To provide materials in all formats to support the instructional, research, and service functions of the University, maintaining a balance appropriate for this user community between ownership of information resources and access to resources owned by others.

2. To provide optimum bibliographic control of the Library's own collections and other appropriate resources.

3. To maintain accurate and efficient records for locating and circulating the Library's own materials.

4. To facilitate access to information resources outside the Library.

5. To take advantage of collaborative arrangements with other entities.

6. To promote understanding of the Library's research capabilities and to encourage the use of its resources and services.

7. To provide instructional programs to enable patrons to use information resources effectively.

8. To provide audiovisual equipment and support for classroom instruction and University functions.

B. Collections: To select, acquire, and maintain materials in all formats to support the instructional, research, and. service functions of the University.

1. To ensure that the collections are relevant to the needs of the Library's users.

2. To establish and implement policies and procedures that contribute to the physical preservation of the collections.

3. To establish and implement policies and procedures that ensure the security of the collections.

C. Facilities: To provide space, equipment, and technology that will ensure operational efficiency, enhance collection preservation, and respond to changing needs of users and staff.

1. To ensure that library space effective accommodates the demands of emerging electronic technologies.

2. To ensure that library space is being used to support the library's stated mission and goals.

3. To provide a safe, clean, and positive work environment for staff and users alike.

D. Personnel: to attract, retain, and develop the best qualified staff possible in order to carry out the mission and goals of the Library.

1. To provide adequate training for all staff to be able to do their jobs well.

2. To provide opportunity and incentive for professional development for all staff members.

3. To enhance staff productivity and morale.

4. To ensure that the Library has the proper person in the proper staff position.

5. To ensure that library positions are appropriately defined and appropriately distributed among the various departments and programs.

E. Administration: To ensure the carrying out of the Library's mission and goals.

1. To enhance the promotion, interpretation, and support of the Library through the development of constructive relationships with the University administration, academic departments, students, and the Library's public in general.

2. To promote communication and cooperation within and among all departments of the Library.

3. To coordinate effectively the programs and resources of the Library.

4. To plan and develop strategies for enhancing the programs and resources of the Library.

5. To solicit and secure the financial support necessary for the continuation and expansion of operations of the Library.

6. To administer the Library's budget and promote optimum use of its financial resources.

7. To ensure that regular and systematic assessment of library activities, programs, departments, and staff is carried out.

05/05/95

URSULINE COLLEGE

RALPH M. BESSE LIBRARY

Mission

The purpose of the Ralph M. Besse Library is to support the mission of Ursuline College by creating a learning environment in the liberal arts tradition in which the intellectual, aesthetic, psychological, physical and spiritual dimensions of life can be integrated to prepare students to serve the community and their professions with distinction and integrity. Ursuline College's primary thrust is the education of women for roles of responsibility and leadership in society. A primary focus of the institution is on excellence in teaching and learning, in a community with a distinctively Ursuline character. The College serves students with a wide range of ages and economic, social, academic and religious backgrounds. Respect for the learning needs of the individual student is emphasized. Flexible scheduling and a variety of approaches to learning are provided to meet the diverse needs of these students. Ursuline College also serves the broader community by offering programs and facilities for social, cultural and spiritual enrichment.

The library reflects the mission of the College by serving the diverse needs of each student, maintaining patron service as its ultimate goal. Using the latest technologies, the library acquires, organizes, maintains and provides access to the information and materials needed by the members of the Ursuline College community for the successful pursuit of their academic goals. The College's curriculum serves as the essential criterion in determining the library's collection and services. A skilled library staff enhances student learning by providing information literacy instruction to promote a valuable lifelong competency.

WABASH COLLEGE LIBRARY MISSION STATEMENT

The mission of the Wabash College Library is to promote the ability to find, evaluate and use library resources in the full exercise of freedom of inquiry that is an integral part of the education of students in the liberal arts and sciences. To meet this mission, the library develops and maintains collections and services that support the mission statement of Wabash College, fostering, in particular, the information literacy skills that are critical to independent intellectual inquiry and life-long learning.

Collections

Our primary guiding collection development principle is to acquire and maintain materials, regardless of format, which are appropriate for students doing research related to their studies and for faculty in preparing their courses.

Given that primary goal, it is the responsibility of the library staff, in conjunction with the faculty:

a) to acquire and maintain a quality on-campus collection of materials that meet the needs of our students;

b) to provide access to information sources that the library does not own by negotiating and maintaining cooperative arrangements with other educational institutions for sharing resources and with commercial content providers, within current legal restrictions on the use of such sources.

A secondary collection development goal is to support faculty scholarship. Such support will be facilitated by acquiring the basic materials faculty need to carry on research, within the resources available, and by providing access to other collections through cooperative use agreements and interlibrary loan.

As a depository for federal government publications, the library is committed to making such documents available to the residents of Montgomery County and other citizens of the Seventh Indiana Congressional District.

The Robert T. Ramsay, Jr., Archival Center will acquire and preserve the records of the college, related materials that document its history, and special collections.

Additionally, the library will assess the need for library materials and services to support non-curricula research and recreational use and will establish priorities for such as financial resources are available.

Services

The library staff will maintain communications with all segments of the college community to promote understanding of library policies and programs, to understand the needs of our users, and to facilitate awareness of developments in library collections and services which have future implications for the library's continued effective support of the curriculum.

The reference and electronic resources librarian will develop and carry out, with faculty colleagues, an instructional program that will foster students' information literacy so they may accomplish their academic goals and have the necessary library skills to support life-long learning.

Under the direction of the reference and electronic resources librarian, library staff will offer reference services for the college community and Montgomery County patrons that allows each user to obtain the information he or she is seeking.

The coordinator of media services and the archivist will provide user services appropriate to the materials in their areas.

The catalog librarian, with the assistance of other library staff, will create bibliographical records, in accordance with cataloging standards, for materials in all formats in the Wabash collection and establish and maintain electronic links to off-campus sources so that users can easily identify materials pertinent to their needs.

The library staff will maintain user policies and procedures for circulation of items from the general collections, interlibrary loan, media and archives which allow fair and equitable access for users, while protecting the physical conditions of these collections.

Ensuring collections and services

Recognizing that the library's success depends on hiring and keeping highly qualified and motivated staff, personnel policies will be written and personnel practices undertaken that will foster each staff member's abilities to meet the mission of the library. Development opportunities will also be provided so that staff may become even more effective contributors to that mission. The head librarian will see that there is qualified staff in sufficient numbers to meet the demands for services.

2

The head librarian will ensure that facilities are adequate to house and preserve the collections; that space and environment allow both users and staff to work productively; and that equipment and systems used to carry out the programs of the library are equal to the tasks we need to accomplish.

The head librarian, in concert with library staff colleagues and with advice from the faculty/student advisory committee, will advocate to the administration a budget that is sufficient to meet the mission of the library in support of the academic program and will administer the dollars allocated for the maximum benefit of the College's educational program. Furthermore, the head librarian will work with college development staff to gain additional sources of support for the library's mission.

<u>Assessment and Review</u>

An annual review of this mission statement and current policies supporting that statement will be conducted by the head librarian, with the assistance of the library staff and the faculty/student library advisory committee.

The library staff will conduct periodic assessments of the quality of the collections and services available to our patrons.

Written October 1997

MISSION STATEMENT

Peterson Memorial Library is a learning environment that responds to the traditional values of the College and to the realities of modern technology. Therefore, the Library fosters the pursuit of knowledge, intellectual and ethical integrity, excellence in teaching and learning, respect for inquiry and diverse points of view, and dedication to service. The Library collects books, periodicals, multimedia, electronic and other resources. It also provides connections to global information networks to enhance the curriculum and assist research. As a locus where information is gathered, organized, and prepared for redistribution, the Library provides members of the College community a place for interaction, consultation, study, instruction, and reflection. Librarians and staff are dedicated to serving the information needs of students and faculty on the main campus, at satellite campuses, and at remote locations.

Library service is essential to the College's educational mission of encouraging the intellectual development of faculty and students. Librarians and staff support the College in this mission by:

- creating and providing the tools that provide access to universal knowledge

- teaching library research skills and the critical evaluation and synthesis of information

- developing, organizing, and maintaining a collection of resources supporting the curriculum of the college, intellectual freedom, and cultural exploration

- offering the College expertise on changing patterns in the creation, organization, and distribution of knowledge.

- cooperating with other area libraries in providing information resources to the Walla Walla valley and Pacific Northwest.

Washington & Lee University

James G. Leyburn Library
_____

MISSION STATEMENT

The University Library serves the student body as a learning and research facility; the faculty as a research facility and a source of contemporary information in his or her own field and parallel disciplines; and the public as a cultural component of the greater university community.

The library has a fundamental role to play in supporting the educational mission of Washington and Lee University by the following means:

     o Maintaining the excellence of its collections, carefully chosen from the wealth of available materials in a variety of formats -- print, audio, video, manuscript, microform, and electronic -- that support the curriculum and promote independent research and original scholarship,

     o Fostering a skilled and dedicated staff, sufficient in number, who are alert to the needs of students and faculty, who can confidently guide them in the discriminating use of the available research tools, who can create and maintain the appropriate records to promote easy access to information,

     o Providing formal and informal instruction in research skills to equip students with the tools to ensure their lifelong intellectual process, and

     o Incorporating the best technology into the operation of the library and employing it to enhance learning.

     The library's other major role is to support the cultural life of the university and extended community by providing a convivial environment that stimulates exploration and discussion of a wide range of topics for intellectual growth and pleasure.

     The challenge to an academic library as we enter the 21st century is to navigate the quickly changing technological landscape with thoughtful study and consideration in order to provide the best overall service to its patrons.

3/3/98

http://www.wlu.edu/~library/leyburn/mission.html

Private Institutions

Over 2500 Students

LIBRARY STRATEGIC PLAN
12/97

MISSION STATEMENT

It is the mission of the Solomon R. Baker Library to support the curricular, co-curricular, service and research needs of Bentley students, faculty and staff by selecting, acquiring and assisting in access to a wide variety of information resources. The Library is central to the mission of the College in providing both a physical and a virtual information center, putting into the hands or onto the computer screens of the entire Bentley community the information resources necessary for learning as well as for their intellectual and cultural development. It is also the role of the Library to ensure that its patrons are instructed in the use, interpretation and ethical treatment of these information sources so that they may bring to the learning process the ability to judge critically the structure and content of these diverse sources.

VISION

The Library is a vital and integral part of the Bentley educational experience, providing needed information resources of the highest quality. The Library will continue to be the leader in delivering information to the campus, working with faculty and other libraries to identify and provide access to resources in support of the curricular, service and research needs of the College. To optimize the quantity and quality of information resources available to the campus the Library will continue to develop strategic alliances with other libraries such as the Webnet Consortium, the Boston Library Consortium, and the Metrowest Massachusetts Regional Library System, in pursuit of advantageous reciprocal use and borrowing arrangements as well as cooperative purchasing of expensive resources.

The issues that all libraries are currently and will continue to deal with involve an increasingly complex 'Mix of collections, access, technology, and media, requiring an increasingly knowledgeable versatile staff of professionals and paraprofessionals to resolve. The Library will need to continue its commitment to the on-going hiring, training and development of skilled, experienced professional staff to ensure the highest most up to date level of knowledge of content and delivery systems of the many available information resources.

Professional librarians have always considered teaching library research methods one of the primary goals of an academic library; currently, however, due to the proliferation of unevaluated raw data available to students electronically, the level of teaching and training required to help them understand and critically evaluate that information will require increasingly more professional time and more expensive training resources than ever before.

Finally, the Library will continue to respond to changes in the ways students other users use the library building so as to ensure its continued vital role in academic and campus life.

With the following strategic initiatives in place the College can expect better-informed, more technologically capable students who will be able to take their place in the business world with abilities and understanding beyond their peers. The College will also have a technologically proficient faculty for whom using academic information technology is a natural part of teaching and research.

MISSION STATEMENT

The Library's mission is to support the educational process of Bradley University:

> Through its collection and its ability to access other Collections, the Library undergirds faculty research and the independent curricular work of students.

> Through its bibliographic instruction programs and the individual work of reference librarians, the Library provides training in using the collection and in assessing what is available and needed from collections not at Bradley.

> Through its building space with study areas, equipment of various kinds, electronic access, reserve and reference and browsing areas, the Library fosters an atmosphere of learning.

> Through the work of the staff it makes its material accessible through a system of organization, shelf arrangements, and catalogs.

Secondarily, the Library's mission is to share with the community its resources through both interlibrary loan and open access to our building and its collections.

1991

College of St. Catherine Libraries/Audio-Visual Services
St. Paul and Minneapolis Campuses

Mission Statement

The mission of the Saint Catherine Libraries/Audio-Visual Services Department is to acquire, organize, provide access to information and academic resources, instruct users, and provide appropriate technology and services in support of the College's mission to educate individuals, especially women,

General Objectives

1. To select, acquire and organize material resources in appropriate formats to support all the programs of the college.

2. To provide effective instruction and services that are responsive to students' needs, locations, schedules and learning styles.

3. To obtain and deliver instructional media and use technology that is adaptable, expandable and compatible with national and international standards,

4. To supply knowledgeable, well-trained personnel to deliver services.

5. To provide supportive, secure, well-maintained facilities conducive to the use and preservation of collections and delivery of service.

6. To collaborate with CLIC and with other public and private entities in providing resources and learning opportunities.

7. To evaluate resources, services and facilities on a regular basis in order to become more effective and efficient.

3/12/96

/mission1.lib

Lesley College

ELEANOR DeWOLFE LUDCKE LIBRARY

Mission Statement

The Ludcke Library provides members of the Lesley College community with access to information in their academic pursuits and the means by which they can make effective use of this information. The library creates an environment that encourages a quest for knowledge and the development of skills for lifelong learning. The library's collections and services support the college in its mission to integrate academic and field-based learning.

In support of this mission, the library has the following goals:

To develop and organize a collection of print and non-print materials that meet the identified and anticipated needs of its users.

To provide services in support of the college's programs both on and off campus.

To provide a staff with appropriate expertise and of sufficient size to assist users in making effective use of the library collections, services, and facilities.

To provide facilities of sufficient size and quality.

To promote resource sharing and cooperative arrangements with other libraries and information services.

To explore and adopt new information technologies.

To interpret library services to students, faculty, administrators and to our extended community.

June 1993

Mission Statement

The Oberlin College community is strongly committed to excellence in teaching, learning, artistry, and research. The Library actively responds to this commitment by providing resources and services that support and enhance the broad and rigorous programs in the College of Arts and Sciences and the Conservatory of Music.

An integral part of the College's academic life, the Library builds and maintains extensive, carefully-selected, and well-organized collections that are essential for the success of the curriculum; it provides wide and effective access to networked scholarly resources; and it works in cooperation with faculty to develop in Oberlin College students competence in using the Library and other information sources. To enable faculty and students to take full advantage of library resources, the Library maintains a highly-qualified staff that is responsive to individual needs and exceptionally dedicated to service and teaching.

http://www.oberlin.edu/~library/services/administrative/mission.html

MISSION OF THE ST. OLAF COLLEGE LIBRARIES

The St Olaf College Libraries serve the College community by providing access to a universe of information, knowledge, and art and by providing systematic instruction in the retrieval and evaluation of information from its many sources. As teaching Libraries we offer active support for the College mission of stimulating critical thinking and lifelong learning, and for the College curriculum, committed to the liberal arts, a global perspective, and rooted in the Christian Gospel

At St. Olaf College, library instruction compliments classroom teaching. St. Olaf has a nationally recognized course-integrated bibliographic instruction program. Through bibliographic instruction and additional one-to one work with reference librarians, students learn to design effective research strategies and evaluate information tools and sources. From the most recent scholarship to items over four centuries old, from a historically strong book collection to an emerging multimedia collection, the libraries seek to mirror the breadth and depth of the undergraduate curriculum and faculty interests through a variety of carefully selected and maintained materials. We provide consistent and finely-tuned access to our collections through adherence to national cataloging standards coupled with a flexible and powerful integrated online catalog.

In an era of complex interaction between electronic, print, and other information sources, our commitment to technological currency provides increasing depth of access to our own collections and timely access to the universe of information outside the College. Our partnership with the Academic Computing Center helps us provide the campus with access to regional, national, and international networks, databases, and other sources of information. Through participation in library networks and consortia we contribute to national and international bibliographic databases; through our interlibrary loan program we share our resources with other libraries and gain access to collections near and far.

Essential to the success to the libraries' mission is an informed and dedicated library faculty and staff committed to excellence in our work and collegial management and participatory decision-making in our governance. The position of College Librarian rotates among the library faculty. The College Librarian and library faculty work together to establish policy in active consultation with library staff, Faculty and staff are encouraged to participate in a wide range of professionals activities from attending workshops to contributing to scholarly publications; many hold leadership positions in local and national organizations.

The future will bring change to our libraries and to our profession. In particular, the variety of information available to us and the media and sources through which we access that information will change, as will College expectations of our role in providing that access. We look forward to integrating new opportunities technology will provide into the Libraries' programs while maintaining our traditionally high standards of instruction and service., To ensure our capacity for this integration, we support continual professional development; in seeking new colleagues, we look for the same mix of excellence, active curiosity, and the demonstrated ability to adapt thoughtfully to new situations we expect of ourselves. As the paradigms of the academic library change, the St. Olaf Libraries will synthesize important change, always adapting with sensitivity to the unique needs of the St. Olaf College community.

Approved by the Library Faculty on 5/94, and by the Dean of the College in a memo dated 6/22/94

SMITH COLLEGE LIBRARIES
STATEMENT OF MISSION

The Smith College Libraries develop and promote access to recorded knowledge in support of the mission of Smith College to "provide the finest possible liberal arts education for undergraduate women." The Libraries strive to provide information services, and resources in all formats, to meet the needs of the undergraduate and graduate curricula, faculty research, administrative support, and the intellectual life of Smith and the Five College community. The Smith College Libraries are also committed to maintaining substantial historical materials and nationally recognized special collections, which serve both scholars and undergraduates. As multimedia, electronic and network technologies evolve, the Smith College Libraries will continue to participate actively in their development and integration for campus-wide information access. Library staff advance the educational purposes of the College through instruction and interpretation for the identification, organization, use and evaluation of information resources. The Libraries endeavor to sustain an environment for staff and library users that ensures respect, diversity, fairness, growth and excellence.

+++++++++++++++++++++++

STATEMENT OF GOALS

These goals expand upon the general mission and cover the major service aims of the libraries' operations. Each section within the library may develop specific objectives related to meeting particular goals, and may analyze its work within this framework.

I.   Developing strong information and research resources.

1.   Responsibly select and acquire resources in all subjects and formats to support the curriculum and faculty research, and to enrich the intellectual environment of library users.

2.   Organize and manage collections and other information resources (regardless of where located) by providing appropriate forms of bibliographic access.

3.   Promote the preservation of library materials where both feasible and desirable to ensure the availability of the collections for future users, through measures such as conservation, reformatting, replacement and environmental controls.

4.   Ensure the continued development and utilization of specialized collections that are distinctive to Smith College and are of national, historic or scholarly interest.

5.   Participate in regional and national resource sharing and other cooperative efforts to enhance access to information and to further the efficient development of local resources.

Smith College

__Providing effective library services.__

1. Provide reference and instructional services to maximize understanding and use of the full scope of information resources, and to foster an inviting, supportive and collaborative learning environment for the Libraries' diverse constituencies.

2. Facilitate access to library materials at Smith and elsewhere through services including on-site use, circulation, course reserves, maintenance of the stacks, interlibrary loan, document delivery and electronic information services.

3. Provide a range of services designed for specific curricular and research needs through professionally staffed branch libraries, multimedia facilities, and other special collections.

4. Promote awareness, understanding and use of the Smith College Libraries through exhibits, publications, publicity, outreach, donor relations and other communication mechanisms.

III. __Maintaining an appropriate physical and technological infrastructure.__

1. Actively monitor developments in computing, networking, and information technology and strive to implement such technologies so as to enhance the quality and cost-effectiveness of library staff operations and patron services.

2. Work closely with other departments at Smith College and the Five Colleges that provide computing, communications, media and facilities support services to ensure integrated and effective mechanisms for access to information resources at the campus, regional and national level.

3. Maintain the physical facilities and equipment necessary for the proper housing, processing, preservation and utilization of library materials in all formats, and for the dynamic provision of the full range of information services.

4. Strive to guarantee and promote an attractive, comfortable, healthful and safe environment for work and study by both users and staff.

IV. __Managing a responsive and responsible workplace.__

1. Organize and administer library operations through effective planning, evaluating and budgeting.

2. Promote the recruitment and development of a talented and motivated staff by providing resources for training, encouraging participation in professional and college activities, and fostering ongoing individual assessment.

3. Encourage communication, participation and innovation through formal and informal opportunities and flexible organizational structures.

4. Adhere to recognized library, academic, and workplace standards that address technical, operational, service, legal and ethical issues.

Adopted by the Staff Council of the Smith College Libraries, May 25, 1993.

© Smith College Libraries, 1993.

84 Private Institutions

MISSION OF THE EUNICE AND JAMES L. WEST LIBRARY
TEXAS WESLEYAN UNIVERSITY

The mission of the West Library is to provide information, both print and non-print, as needed by members of the University community for the successful pursuit of its many and varied programs. The Library affords students the opportunity to augment classroom experiences with independent learning and encourages reading for recreation and general information. The Library is also responsible for accessing useful information, techniques, and technology from the library, information, and education professions to meet needs and improve services. Additionally, the Library provides instruction for the development of life-long library user skills.

GOALS OF THE EUNICE AND JAMES L. WEST LIBRARY
TEXAS WESLEYAN UNIVERSITY

- To supply and maintain a range and quality of services which support, enhance and promote the academic program of the University.

- To facilitate Library staff participation in continuing education and professional opportunities.

- To collect and maintain the historical records of the institution.

- To support the Library Bill of Rights of the American Library Association.

- To encourage library use.

- To supply resources that will adequately meet the needs of ability challenged students.

- Strengthen the information resources (print and non-print) budget to more adequately support Texas Wesleyan University academic programs (e.g. grants, broaden financial base).

- To adhere to the American Library Association Code of Ethics - adopted June 28, 1995.

Collins Memorial Library
Mission Statement

Collins Memorial Library is a key intellectual resource and a leader in information technology for the University of Puget Sound. More than a collection or a building, our services are designed to support students, faculty and staff in their efforts to develop the skills and strengths needed to pursue intellectual challenges and success in a changing world. To this end we emphasize:

- collaborating with faculty to provide opportunities for students to identify their personal information needs, to locate desired information in a variety of formats, and to critically evaluate the information found

- assisting users in understanding the applications, strengths, and weaknesses of varied information delivery systems

- facilitating maximum access with minimal delay to information

- providing and designing easy access to an array of ideas and information available through world-wide resources

- selecting and maintaining a core collection of literature and materials important to an undergraduate education in the liberal arts and to graduate education in occupational and physical therapy and education

Librarians and staff alike will continue to evaluate and review services for effectiveness and to apply technology when possible to improve service.

Revised 1/98

UNIVERSITY OF RICHM0ND LIBRARIES

CENTRAL LIBRARY - BOATWRIGHT MEMORIAL LIBRARY
BUSINESS INFORMATION CENTER, MEDIA RESOURCE CENTER
SCIENCE LIBRARY, MUSIC LIBRARY
LAW LIBRARY

VISION

All members of the university community will have access to a variety of information sources from their classrooms, residence halls, offices, and homes for their academic, professional and intellectual development. The Libraries and Media Resource Center will ensure that all members of the university community possess the skills to become information literate to participate as global citizens in the information society.

MISSION

The Libraries and Media Resource Center will enable students, faculty, staff, and the university community to exploit materials and electronic sources for their academic and intellectual endeavors by developing collections of breadth and depth; by facilitating comprehensive access to information through the use of emerging technologies; by providing instruction for the effective use of all resources; and by maintaining state-of-the-art facilities.

York College of Pennsylvania

Schmidt Library
York College of Pennsylvania

Susan M. Campbell
Library Director

Mission and Goals

It is the mission of Schmidt Library to provide access to recorded knowledge through materials, services, and equipment which support the career-oriented liberal arts curriculum of York College of Pennsylvania. To that end, the Library Faculty and Staff will:

1. work with other faculty members to develop well rounded collections of print and non-print materials to support all facets of the curriculum.

2. acquire, process, and organize all materials for efficient user access; provide means of access to these materials, as well as to those not owned by Schmidt Library; and maintain all collections and equipment in good condition.

3. teach students to become knowledgeable, confident, self-sufficient Library users through desk assistance, orientation, and classroom library instruction.

4. provide online searching to support faculty teaching and research; and develop and promote programs to introduce online searching to students.

5. recruit and train personnel whose knowledge and skills facilitate the Library's mission; encourage Staff development at all levels; and systematically evaluate the performance of all individuals.

6. develop budget requests to support the continuing growth of all collections, provide all necessary equipment, and maintain all services.

7. maintain open forums of communication within the Library; use a Library newsletter, the Library handbooks for faculty and students, discussions with the Faculty Senate Library Committee, and other means to keep users informed and to gather information; and maintain an awareness of College developments which might have an impact on the Library.

88 Private Institutions

Mission and Goals - page 2

8. provide adequate facilities and an appropriate environment for users, staff, collections, and equipment.

9. continue to foster interlibrary cooperation and resource sharing to provide users with materials not available in Schmidt Library.

10. support an integrated, automated library system and promote knowledge of current developments in information technology.

11. ensure availability of equipment which is easy to use and which is standardized when possible within format to facilitate user recognition.

12. maintain audio visual production facilities and provide production materials at minimum or no cost to users.

13. maintain the archival documents and historical records of York County Academy, York Collegiate Institute, York Junior College, and York College of Pennsylvania.

14. preserve collections to insure that important resources are available to future users.

15. promote knowledge and information and take an active role in the intellectual life of the College through sponsorship of exhibits, lectures, and other programs.

16. examine and revise policies and procedures to provide accurate, prompt, and friendly service.

17. examine these goals regularly and revise them as necessary.

September 1994

Public Institutions

Under 2500 Students

ATHENS STATE COLLEGE LIBRARY

Mission Statement

The mission of the Athens State College Library is to identify, acquire, maintain, preserve, and provide access to information and research in support of academic programs offered by the college; to enhance bibliographic skills of patrons through instruction; to work cooperatively with faculty and the greater community to build appropriate collections in a variety of formats; to respond to advances in information technology; to establish and maintain cooperative agreements for resource sharing with other libraries; and, to encourage research and life-long learning.

04/21/98

Public Institutions

Over 2500 Students

**California State University, San Marcos
Library & Information Services
Mission Statement**

Library and Information Services (LIS) is committed to providing a learning environment which supports the information needs of the CSUSM community. Our services, collections, teaching, and community outreach honor and reflect diverse perspectives, learning styles and ways of knowing. With the help of innovative technologies, our staff aggressively select, acquire, provide access and deliver resources and instruction that support the life-long learning needs of our students and community. LIS upholds and practices the principles of the CSUSM Mission Statement and the Library Bill of Rights, endorsed by the American Library Association.

rev. 4/98

*This is the CSUSM Library and Information Services mission statement as of May, 1998.

California University of Pennsylvania

Introduction

Changes in library resources and use have been dramatic since the last Middle States visitation. The emergence of library materials on CD-ROM prior to 1990 has evolved to the availability of electronic databases directly accessible via the Internet in 1998. This is dramatically reflected in how the library is used, its resources, and almost every facet of its operation.

Mission Statement

The mission of the Louis L. Manderino Library is to support the goals and objectives of California University of Pennsylvania through effective organization of materials and electronic resources. The Library's role is to provide resources, instruction, and services to meet the educational, recreational, and research needs of faculty, students, alumni, and community patrons within the region.

The Library's goals are:

1. To support the undergraduate and graduate instructional programs of the University, as well as provide for the research, educational, and recreational needs of the University community.
2. To organize the library's resources in such a manner as to make bibliographic access to materials manageable for users.
3. To provide optimum access to resources via reference services, bibliographic instruction, the Internet, electronic databases, interlibrary loan, etc.
4. To provide an environment that is conducive for the implementation of the library's goals and objectives.
5. To assure that the library is sufficiently staffed by professional and support personnel so as to maximize the effective implementation of the library's program.
6. To insure that the library is consistently funded at a level that allows for proper planning and continuous resource growth.

University Libraries	

Mission of Clarion University Libraries

The mission of the Clarion University Libraries, comprised of the Carlson Library on the Clarion campus and Suhr Library on the Venango campus, is to:

- assist University undergraduate and graduate students, faculty, staff, and administration in conveniently locating and accessing the University's information resources and those of other sources;

- develop and provide timely and responsive services, programs, and tools that facilitate translation of information into knowledge and support research, scholarship, teaching, and learning;

- build, select, and preserve, in cooperation with University faculty, a collection of information resources commensurate with the current and anticipated discipline needs of the University's instructional programs and supportive of teaching and learning processes;

- contribute to progress of the University and the profession; and

- participate in addressing the information resource needs of local and rural communities in Pennsylvania.

http://www.clarion.edu/library/mission.htm

Public Institutions 99

B.   The EWU Libraries Mission Statement

EWU Libraries support the instructional and research mission of the University through the development of on-site collections, access to off-site resources, personalized assistance in the use of library and information resources, and instruction on research strategies and tools. Our mission is stated as follows:

The mission of the University Libraries is to ensure that the students of EWU have access to information and ideas essential to achieving a high quality education at Eastern Washington University.

The Libraries will provide information services and library materials in such a way as to uphold intellectual freedom, promote information literacy and encourage lifelong learning.

The Libraries will support high quality undergraduate education with services and primarily on-site collections; provide graduate education with on-site services and collections as well as access to remote research materials; and support faculty research largely through access to off-site resources.

C.   The EWU Libraries' Vision

The EWU Libraries promote the University's vision for providing top quality baccalaureate and graduate education. Through carefully selected and organized collections, advanced information technologies, and responsive services to EWU students, faculty and staff and to members of our broader communities, we contribute to the intellectual, cultural and economic vitality of the Inland Northwest. Our faculty and staff work aggressively with others in the University and throughout the state and nation to ensure that our students and faculty have the best resources at hand, either on our shelves or quickly accessible from another library or electronic source. Through innovation and assessment, we continually improve our resources and services to meet the changing needs of our users, to make effective use of new technologies, and to retain the most useful traditional resources.

We actively support a superior learning environment and the development of students' critical thinking skills through instructional programs focusing on retrieval and evaluation of information and changing information technologies.

Believing that critical thinking and successful problem solving require the ability to find and evaluate pertinent information, our class instruction and services to individuals stress clear definition of problems and queries and evaluation of documents and information retrieved.

Believing that successful lifelong learning requires the individual to develop self confidence in his/her ability to pursue individual inquiries, we provide quality personalized research assistance to individuals.

Believing that success in information seeking is influenced by personal learning style and availability of appropriate research tools and facilities, we provide students and faculty with the opportunity to develop expertise in using traditional sources and advanced information technologies.

We encourage our students to recognize the importance of libraries and other information providers in their continuing intellectual and professional development and to become lifelong supporters of the EWU Libraries and the libraries in their communities and workplaces.

Mission Statement

In affirmation of Henderson State University's mission as Arkansas's public liberal arts university, the mission of Huie Library is:

- To provide information resources and services that implement, support, and enrich the academic programs of the parent institution;
- To facilitate the interaction of students and faculty with the ever expanding, increasingly complex information universe;
- To support and assist faculty efforts to instill in students an ability to recognize a need for information, to understand the value of information, and to distinguish between information and knowledge.
- To serve as teachers, mediators, liaisons, advisors, consultants, and partners in the information seeking-process.
- To encourage the habit of reading and use of libraries in order to develop the potential for self education and intellectual development for lifelong learning.

Last Updated April 20, 1998

URL: http://www.hsu.edu/dept/lib/info/mission.htm

**Kutztown University
Rohrbach Library**

Mission:

To be the central campus information resource, and a companion source for local, regional, state, national and international users.

To be a dynamic academic system devoted to programs and services which emphasize the investigative and information management skills of locating, evaluating, organizing, using, and presenting information.

Principles:

1. The Library is an intellectual environment. It organizes and offers information to complement the curricula. It provides learning opportunities for users to augment classroom experience, to inspire independent learning, to reach intellectual and academic independence, and to gain personal enrichment.

2. The Library plays an integral role in the academic process. It supports faculty with their research and classroom information needs. It provides students with instruction that strengthens critical thinking and information retrieval skills, providing a foundation for lifelong learning.

3. The library critically selects the information it acquires to uphold the mission of the university. It endorses the American Library Association's Bill of Rights while continuing to operate within an intellectual freedom model.

4. Quality service is ensured by the accessibility to professionally trained staff, capable of providing prompt response to information needs.

5. The Library is committed to maintaining efficient, effective information management regardless of where the information is located or in what format it appears.

6. The Library is continually searching to best utilize the most appropriate technology or medium for managing the ever-evolving state of information.

2/96

SOUTHERN OREGON UNIVERSITY

LIBRARY MISSION STATEMENT

The SOU library participates in the teaching and learning mission of Southern Oregon University by selecting, organizing, and maintaining collections and providing access to global information resources in support of a dynamic curriculum. The Library stimulates, guides and mentors students, faculty and community members in developing lifelong skills in critical thinking and information literacy. The SOU Library faculty and staff respond creatively to rapidly evolving information technologies and resources and are committed to excellent instruction and service in both traditional and electronic resources. The Library environment is conducive to independent thinking, research, and learning with materials representing diverse perspectives and formats.

9/25/96
Approved by Library Advisory Committee 5/9/97

SOUTHERN OREGON STATE COLLEGE LIBRARY

VISION STATEMENT

We, the faculty and staff of the SOSC Library, envision a library based on excellence of service, innovation, meeting the information needs of students and faculty, and serving as an intellectual resource to southern Oregon. The library provides leadership to our region in these endeavors. Within the library there is a collegial environment of mutual respect of values, philosophies, experiences, and commitments.

An expanded physical facility is welcoming , user friendly, and is well designed for people, services, and.-access to collections. The library provides an environment of study, contemplation, investigation, discussion, and artistic expression.

The collection development policy serves the instructional mission of the college and gives librarians selection responsibility in their subject areas. The collection respects and reflects all cultures, beliefs, and lifestyles, and is not limited to specific formats. Collection building is based upon an internal collection development policy and collection development coordination among OSSHE and regional libraries.

Technology enhances learning, drawing knowledge and information from throughout the nation and world. Access and delivery of information to on-campus and extended campus users is based on traditional and electronic resources, including remote databases, e-mail, electronic document delivery, World Wide Web, and state-of-the-art technologies.

The library's instruction programs, services, and information resources are integral to the college curriculum. Close instructional partnerships between librarians and other faculty emphasize critical thinking and subject-based teaching. Our active outreach programs promote services to diverse groups.

September 1993, revised November 1996

SWOSU Library Mission Statement

The Library supports the University's mission to insure quality education, enable student development and serve as a cultural and educational resource for western Oklahoma. This support is offered through organized materials and services, support of courses and individual research. The Library provides opportunities for students to obtain skills, knowledge and cultural appreciation that lead to effective life-long use of information, productive lives and effective citizenship.

Al Harris Library Long Range Program, 1994-1999

There are several changes in the library environment which will impact library services and systems in the next few years. These include 1) increasing amounts of full text material in electronic form: from the publisher, Internet or other sources, 2) ever increasing availability of table of contents services and of journal article information through indexes and abstracts, 3) increasing demand from users for remote electronic access to all library resources, 4) increasing demand from handicapped users to equal access to all library materials, 5) increasing cooperation among the larger libraries in the state and the resultant sharing of resources, 6) the trend to provide materials "in time" rather than "in case".

```
MISSION STATEMENT
COLLEGE LIBRARIES
SUNY POTSDAM
```

The Potsdam College Libraries support the mission of Potsdam College by developing collections and services that make the Libraries integral to the learning process, both within and beyond the classroom. In so doing, the libraries strive:

* to promote information literacy among the college community as a necessary pre-requisite to success in an increasingly complex and technological world;

* to provide access to resources that reflect a broad range of perspectives, viewpoints, and approaches;

* to incorporate innovative technology wherever appropriate to extend collections and services beyond the physical walls of the library;

* to balance opportunities for off-site access with the need for on-site ownership.

Recognizing that students are their primary clientele, the College Libraries will also seek to support the scholarly and research needs of faculty and staff. The Libraries will, as feasible, extend services to the citizens of the region.

Approved by Planning Committee, 5/26/93
Approved by Library Council, 6/2/93
Reaffirmed by Library Council, 9/6/95

THE UNIVERSITY OF SOUTHERN COLORADO
UNIVERSITY LIBRARY'S MISSION STATEMENT

The University Library's mission is to support teaching, learning, and research throughout the campus
by actively encouraging and facilitating use of its collections and services, and by offering advice, assistance, and training in information skills. To fulfill this mission, the Library:

- provides access to print and audiovisual materials, reference -services, electronic information resources, and interlibrary loan

- helps users develop skills in the effective use of information

- provides a strong public service orientation and an environment conducive to study and research

- develops the collection and allocates library resources in response to user needs

- delivers information using state-of-the-art technologies

- serves the community and regional libraries

- participates with other libraries in resource sharing

- promotes academic freedom by endorsing the Library Bill of Rights, the Freedom to View, and the Freedom to Read

WILLIAM PATTERSON COLLEGE
SARAH BYRD ASKEW LIBRARY

Mission Statement
April 24, 1990

The Library staff of William Paterson College is dedicated to the world of learning and directs its efforts toward the goal of educational excellence. In a real sense the Library is an information center, providing information through traditional and electronic media. Toward this end the staff provides assistance and instruction in the effective use of library-resources and seeks to acquire whatever books, media, software, and other materials members of the College community need for their work and growth. Thus, the staff is committed to support the educational programs of the College by providing a balanced but diverse collection and the broadest possible access to information wherever that information is available.

Such a commitment on the part of the staff requires an understanding of the educational communities of the College. But beyond that, it requires continual personal and professional growth and knowledge about the changes in our society, the resources, and the technology which make possible the best service to the students and staff, of William Paterson College.